D0476095

MOTSON'S
FA CUP ODYSSEY
The World's Greatest Knockout Competition

MOTSON'S

MOTSON'S
FA CUP ODYSSEY
The World's Greatest Knockout Competition

John Motson OBE

ROBSON BOOKS

First published in Great Britain in 2005 by Robson Books, The Chrysalis Building, Bramley Road, London W10 6SP

An imprint of **Chrysalis** Books Group plc

Copyright © 2005 John Motson

Research by Nick Brownlee

The right of John Motson to be identified as the author of this work has been asserted by him in accordance with the Copyright, Designs and Patents Act 1988.

The author has made every reasonable effort to contact all copyright holders. Any errors that may have occurred are inadvertent and anyone who for any reason has not been contacted is invited to write to the publishers so that a full acknowledgement may be made in subsequent editions of this work.

British Library Cataloguing in Publication Data
A catalogue record for this title is available from the British Library.

ISBN 1 86105 903 5

All rights reserved. No part of this publication may be reproduced, stored in a retrieval system, or transmitted in any form or by any means, electronic, mechanical, photocopying, recording or otherwise, without the prior permission in writing of the publishers.

Printed and bound in Italy by ░ Grafica Veneta S.p.A.

— FOREWORD —

My love affair with the FA Cup began when my father, the Rev. William Motson, took me to watch the 1953 final on a friend's television. It was Coronation Year, when Everest was conquered, England regained the Ashes and Gordon Richards finally won the Derby – and a lot of families invested in their first black-and-white television set with the nine-inch screen. Aged seven, I sat transfixed as Stanley Matthews inspired Blackpool's comeback from 3–1 down to beat Bolton 4–3. In those days the small Lancashire towns had big clubs, although it was really Stan Mortensen's day – he got a hat-trick.

By the time Manchester City beat Birmingham three years later, we had our own television at home. Then, for the next five years at boarding school, I somehow found a way of following the final, even if it meant a transistor radio on the cricket field. My dad and I attended my first Wembley final in 1964, when West Ham beat Preston – though he was quick to remind me that he had listened to the first post-war final, between Charlton and his team, Derby County, while rocking me in my pram.

When I joined BBC radio in 1968, my job at the next three finals was as an interviewer – a role I continued in television between 1972 and 1976. I was crouched by the goal when Allan Clarke's header won the Cup for Leeds; held Graham Paddon's winner's medal while he went on the lap of honour after West Ham beat Fulham; and had my glasses knocked off by a flying object as I escorted Lawrie McMenemy down the tunnel with the FA Cup after Second Division Southampton had beaten Manchester United.

After all that, the commentary box high up in the stand seemed rather detached, but the responsibility of bringing the Cup final to the nation never ceased to make me feel humble, nervous and very exposed.

I was lucky enough to be at the BBC microphone for 26 finals between 1977 and 2005. There were also five replays in that period, so since any mistakes I might have made would still have counted against me, I was claiming 31 finals as this book went to press. But everybody knows the glamour and glory of this fantastic competition – the oldest and still the best in the world – does not begin and end with the final. It is the romance of the early rounds that gives the FA Cup its unique flavour.

I will always be associated with Hereford's unlikely victory over Newcastle in 1972 – and am proud to wear that badge. But I also covered Sutton United's triumph over top-division Coventry 17 years later, and was there when York City knocked out Arsenal, and Leatherhead so nearly embarrassed Leicester.

When I started in television, the final was the only game shown live. Now, the BBC screens three live matches in every round once the big clubs enter, as well as midweek replays. My visits to Exeter – who had held Cup holders Manchester United at Old Trafford – and Plymouth were among the highlights of the 2004–05 season.

I have been to eight World Cups, eight European Championships and seen the Champions League grow into a financial monster, but nothing will detract from the democratic appeal of the best Cup competition in the business. I just won't allow it.

The greater part of the work that has gone into this book is by writer Nick Brownlee, who shares with me a fascination for the FA Cup and its history. I hope that this enthusiasm will come across in the pages that follow, and I hope you enjoy the read as much as I have.

John Motson OBE
July 2005

— THE STATISTICIAN'S DREAM FINAL —

The 1980 Cup final between Arsenal and West Ham is best remembered for Trevor Brooking's stooping, headed winner for the Hammers in the 13th minute. Brooking himself was more surprised than anyone that the ball ended up in the net – he claims it was only the third headed goal of his career.

The match itself was not a classic by any means, but all it lacked in technique and finesse for the soccer purist, it more than made up for in juicy nuggets for the statistician. The facts of the matter are:

- Arsenal were the first side to appear in three successive finals in the 20th century.

- Pat Rice of Arsenal was the first player to appear in five finals for one club.

- At 17 years and 256 days Paul Allen of West Ham was the youngest player to appear in a Wembley final.

- Arsenal equalled Newcastle United's record of 11 finals.

- It was only Wembley's third all-London final.

- Arsenal and Liverpool had played out the longest semi-final in Cup history (0 0, 1–1, 1–1, 1–0 – 420 minutes in all).

- West Ham's victory was the third by a Second Division team in eight years.

— JOBSWORTH —

When Barnsley turned up at Crystal Palace stadium for their final against Newcastle in 1910, the team's officials discovered that they had left their special Cup final tickets behind. Thinking that this would not be a problem, they explained their predicament to the commissionaire on the door – and he promptly refused to let them in. The jobsworth relented only when an FA official pointed out that unless he allowed Barnsley into the ground there wouldn't be a final, and 77,747 expectant fans would want to know why.

— ERRANT HUSBAND —

In 1968 West Bromwich Albion celebrated equalling Newcastle's record of appearing in ten FA Cup finals by beating Everton at Wembley.

Jeff Astle's winning goal came three minutes into extra time and maintained his record of scoring in every round – but had it not been for a howler of a miss by Everton's Jimmy Husband the trophy would have been heading for Goodison Park. As he latched on to a cross by team-mate Johnny Morrissey, all Husband had to do was nod the ball into the empty net from six yards. Astonishingly, his header looped up and over the bar.

Astle's goal almost didn't happen either. As he ran towards goal a lunging tackle by Howard Kendall nearly knocked him off his feet. As he regained his balance he hit a right-foot drive which cannoned off Everton defender Colin Harvey. Collecting the rebound, Astle fired a shot with his weaker left foot, and from 20 yards the ball flew into the far corner of the net.

— A HAT-TRICK OF FINALS —

Only four players have appeared in the Cup final for three different clubs. They are: Harold Halse (Manchester United, Aston Villa, Chelsea), Ernie Taylor (Newcastle, Blackpool, Manchester United), John Barnes (Watford, Liverpool, Newcastle) and Dennis Wise (Wimbledon, Chelsea, Millwall).

— CROWD DISTURBANCE —

Terry Phelan never scored a better goal than when he dribbled through almost the entire Tottenham team to net Manchester City's second in the 1993 quarter-final at Maine Road. Unfortunately Spurs had already scored four, and with three minutes remaining City fans decided to take matters into their own hands. As Phelan celebrated, thousands of supporters spilled on to the pitch in a concerted effort to get the match abandoned.

Although there was no violence, there was also no way the game would be declared void. Thirteen mounted police were called on to clear the pitch, ensuring the last minutes could be played out and City's Cup run brought to an end.

— A BAD YEAR —

With the Heysel disaster and the Bradford fire, the 1984–85 season was one to forget, and that year's FA Cup was not spared from the pall of gloom hanging over the English game.

In the sixth round, Luton and Millwall clashed on and off the pitch. In front of several million TV viewers, rival fans spilled on to the pitch armed with ripped-up seats and for 25 minutes police struggled to control the fighting. Some 30 officers were injured before order was restored. Luton won 1–0, but it was a result which paled into insignificance compared to the disgraceful scenes.

The tarnished image of the Cup was not improved during the drab Wembley encounter between Manchester United and Everton three months later, when United's Kevin Moran became the first player to be sent off in a final.

— KIWI FIRST —

Ryan Nelsen became the first New Zealander to appear in an FA Cup semi-final when he played in Blackburn Rovers' 3–0 defeat against Arsenal in 2005.

— APPEARANCES IN THE SEMI-FINAL —

Competition proper 1871–72 to 2004–05:

Team	Appearances
Arsenal	25
Manchester United	24
Everton	23
Liverpool	21
Aston Villa	19
West Bromwich Albion	19
Tottenham Hotspur	17
Blackburn Rovers	17
Newcastle United	17
Sheffield Wednesday	16

— CROWD POWER —

In 1974 Newcastle United reached the FA Cup final for the first time in nearly 20 years, but the road to Wembley was long, winding and pitted with potential upsets.

In the earlier rounds United, boasting the likes of Malcolm Macdonald, Terry McDermott, Terry Hibbitt and Bob Moncur in their line-up, had twice been taken to replays by rank outsiders, non-League Hendon and Scunthorpe United of the Fourth Division.

Having to negotiate such possible banana-skins only two years after they had been turfed out of the Cup by non-League Hereford made many among the Magpies faithful feel it was a miracle that the team had made it to the quarter-final.

Ominously, their opponents at St James's Park were Second Division Nottingham Forest – and Tyneside's worst fears were realised when goals from Ian Bowyer and Liam O'Kane gave Forest a 2–1 lead at half-time. With the second half ten minutes old, all hell broke loose when David Craig fouled Forest's Duncan McKenzie and referee Gordon Kew not only gave a penalty but sent Pat Howard for an early bath for dissent. George Lyall duly converted the spot kick and at 3–1 it seemed the Magpies were heading out of the competition.

At that point around 500 Geordie fans invaded the pitch. Kew took the teams to the dressing rooms, but not before two Forest players had been assaulted. In all, 23 people were taken to hospital and 103 others treated for injuries. The police made 39 arrests.

After a 15-minute absence the teams returned to the pitch and in a hostile atmosphere a clearly shaken Forest collapsed, conceding three goals in the last 20 minutes.

But the saga did not end there. The FA ordered that the match should be replayed at neutral Goodison Park where, after a 0–0 draw, Macdonald scored the only goal in the second replay to settle the tie.

As one observer later pointed out: 'If a home crowd is worth a goal start, then a pitch invasion is worth three.'

As it turned out, three goals was precisely the number by which Liverpool beat Newcastle in the final.

— MARATHON MEN —

They were the two best teams in England and in 1980 Arsenal and Liverpool delivered a marathon semi-final that just ran and ran. Having played out a tense 0–0 draw at Hillsborough, the teams met again a few days later at Villa Park where Alan Sunderland – the last-gasp Gunners hero against Manchester United in the previous year's final – again left it late to equalise David Fairclough's strike. In the second replay it was Liverpool's turn to live on the edge. Sunderland was once more on the mark for Arsenal, this time scoring after a mere 15 seconds, but Kenny Dalglish levelled it for Liverpool with only seconds remaining in injury time at the end of the match.

So it was that the teams faced each other for the fourth time at Coventry's Highfield Road. This time, surely, something had to give – although it took a rare error to conjure the all-important winning goal after 12 minutes.

Defending on the edge of his own six-yard box, Liverpool's normally rock-solid Ray Kennedy inexplicably stood on the ball. It was picked up by the lurking Frank Stapleton, whose neat cross was turned in by Brian Talbot.

Defeat cost Liverpool the chance of the League and FA Cup double and sent Arsenal through to a Wembley final against underdogs West Ham. But the four-game, seven-hour slog had taken its toll and the Gunners tamely surrendered by a single goal to nil.

— WHO, ME? —

The record books show that the 1920 Cup final between Aston Villa and Huddersfield Town was won by a solitary goal by Villa's Billy Kirton. But although he knew there had been a goal, Kirton himself had no idea that he was the scorer. A crowd of players had contested a corner and the ball had flown into the net, but it was not until after the match that the referee confirmed that Kirton had got the final touch.

The controversy did not end there, however. Some 61 years later, Huddersfield's Jack Swann revealed that he thought it was an own-goal by his team-mate Tom Wilson.

— FA CUP VENUES —

Before finding a permanent home at Wembley Stadium, the FA Cup final was played at any sporting ground deemed big enough to stage it – and the FA authorities were not afraid to take the game's showpiece out of the capital.

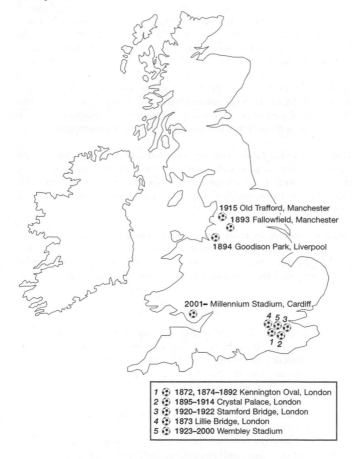

1915 Old Trafford, Manchester
1893 Fallowfield, Manchester
1894 Goodison Park, Liverpool
2001– Millennium Stadium, Cardiff

1 ⚽	1872, 1874–1892 Kennington Oval, London
2 ⚽	1895–1914 Crystal Palace, London
3 ⚽	1920–1922 Stamford Bridge, London
4 ⚽	1873 Lillie Bridge, London
5 ⚽	1923–2000 Wembley Stadium

— ALL CHANGE —

The 1875 final was the last in which the teams exchanged ends after every goal.

— THE MINSTERMEN SHOOT DOWN THE GUNNERS —

A fourth-round tie between Third Division minnows and First Division aristocrats, a frozen pitch, and the *Match of the Day* cameras – it was the perfect scenario for a Cup upset, and in January 1985 that's precisely what happened when York City played host to Arsenal at Bootham Crescent.

Gunners boss Don Howe had splashed out £4.5 million on a team which included stars like Tony Woodcock, Charlie Nicholas, David O'Leary and Paul Mariner; this compared to the £20,000 it had cost Denis Smith to assemble the Minstermen.

But it mattered not, as York tore into their illustrious visitors from the first whistle. Unable to play their cultured passing game on a bone-hard, rutted pitch, Arsenal were rattled throughout – but with 90 minutes on the clock they must have thought they had done enough to earn a replay at Highbury.

Then York striker Keith Houchen was pushed over in the box by Steve Williams, and more than 10,000 fans went wild as the referee pointed to the spot. Houchen, who would score a spectacular Cup final goal for Coventry City two years later, stepped up and coolly despatched the ball past John Lukic.

In the next round, Bootham Crescent nearly became the graveyard for yet another high-flying side. Liverpool were grateful to escape with a 1–1 draw, though four days later the Merseysiders restored a little pride for the top flight by sticking seven past City in the Anfield replay.

— PLEASE, SIR! —

Concerned that his pupils weren't getting enough exercise, in 1872 the headmaster of Donington Grammar School in Lincolnshire hit upon a novel idea – he entered them into the first-ever FA Cup competition. He even enlisted the help of an army sergeant to drill the side to a peak of fitness in preparation for the competition. What he didn't count on was the vagaries of the draw, which pitched them against Glasgow side Queen's Park. Unable to afford the train fare to Scotland, the school had to drop out. They never entered the competition again.

THE MAN WHO INVENTED THE FA CUP
— (AMONG OTHER THINGS) —

Charles William Alcock was the man who invented the FA Cup. And as the fellow who also invented the concept of international matches, and proposed the acceptance of professionalism in the game, it could be argued, too, that he invented modern football as we know it.

Like many of his era, Alcock was a man to whom sport had no boundaries. As well as being secretary of the FA, he was also secretary of Surrey County Cricket Club – which explains why FA Cup finals were played for 21 years at the Kennington Oval.

There he instigated England's first football international (in which he also played), and the first cricket international in 1880. In 1882 he was officiating in the famous Test match between England and Australia in which the Ashes were created.

Not content with football and cricket, Alcock was also instrumental in arranging the first rugby international in England, as well as staging games of hockey, lacrosse and even baseball at the Oval.

When he was not redrawing the boundaries of modern sport, Alcock was a pioneering sports journalist (it was in the offices of his periodical, *The Sportsman*, that the FA Cup was conceived).

As one contemporary writer put it: 'When the flashing meteors have come and gone, when the league tables are full and complete, and when the present fades into the past, the name of C W Alcock will stand out all the more prominently, like a rugged rock in a sea of bubbles.'

— SPURS DEFY THE BAN —

Mired up to their necks in financial irregularities, Tottenham Hotspur were dealt a further blow when in the summer of 1994 the FA took the draconian decision to ban them for one year from Cup competition. They were only reinstated in December 1994 after arguing their case vehemently at a tribunal. Back on track, and inspired by German signing Jurgen Klinsmann, Spurs went all the way to the semi-finals in spring 1995, where they were beaten by Everton, who went on to win the final.

— THE END OF THE WANDERERS —

In the 1870s no-one could touch Wanderers, who won three Cups in a row. But by the end of the decade time was beginning to catch up with their own quaint brand of amateurism. The club prided itself on fielding sides made up from players from other teams, but as their rivals began to take the Cup more seriously they became less inclined to loan out their best players. In 1879 and 1880 the writing was on the wall as they were stuffed by Old Etonians, and in 1881, unable to raise a team, Wanderers were forced to scratch from the tournament they had helped to launch ten years before.

— SIR ALEX GOES FOR PLAN B —

Having abstained from the 1999–2000 FA Cup in favour of an abortive trip to the World Club Championships in Brazil, Manchester United chose to devalue the competition once again five years later when they sent out a second-string side to play Exeter in the third round at Old Trafford.

A combination including youth and reserve team players such as Gerard Pique, Jon Spector, Chris Eagles, David Jones, Liam Miller and Kieran Richardson were played off the park by the Grecians, and although the game finished 0–0, even United boss Sir Alex Ferguson admitted that his side were fortunate to have survived.

'The only positive thing we can take out of the game is that we are still in the competition,' he said. 'This is Exeter's day but I will play a much stronger team in the replay and we will not make this mistake again.'

Sure enough it was a vastly different side which turned out ten days later at St James Park, and two of the returning superstars, Ronaldo and Rooney, bagged the goals which took United through to the fourth round.

As United's League and European campaigns faltered, Sir Alex was glad to have been given a second chance at the Cup, and did not make the same mistake again as his side powered through to the final against Arsenal.

— ABIDE WITH ME —

An ever-present ingredient of every FA Cup final since 1927, 'Abide With Me' was written in 1847 by the Rev. Henry Francis Lyte of All Saints Church, Brixham, Devon. As the words show, it is an incongruously morose hymn for one which has become synonymous with pre-match celebrations. Lyte obviously knew what he was talking about, however – he died just two months after completing it.

> Abide with me; fast falls the eventide
> The darkness deepens; Lord, with me abide
> When other helpers fail and comforts flee
> Help of the helpless, O abide with me
>
> I need Thy presence every passing hour
> What but Thy grace can foil the tempter's power?
> Who like Thyself my guide and stay can be?
> Through cloud and sunshine, Lord, abide with me
>
> Hold Thou Thy Cross before my closing eyes
> Shine through the gloom and point me to the skies
> Heav'n's morning breaks and earth's vain shadows flee
> In life, in death, O Lord abide with me
>
> Swift to its close ebbs out life's little day
> Earth's joys grow dim, its glories pass away
> Change and decay in all around I see
> O Thou who changest not abide with me
>
> I fear no foe with Thee at hand to bless
> Ills have no weight and tears no bitterness
> Where is death's sting? Where grave thy victory?
> I triumph still if Thou abide with me.

— STILL AROUND —

When Blackburn Rovers and West Bromwich Albion met in the Cup final of 1886, a poignant record was created. It was the earliest final between two sides which are still in existence today. By then, pioneers like Wanderers and Royal Engineers had either disbanded or were reaching the end of the line.

— WHERE'S BLY? —

The fourth-round tie between non-League Weymouth and Preston North End in January 1961 was 14 minutes old when thick fog forced the referee to abandon the game. As the teams trooped back to the dressing room, unable to see for more than a few yards, Weymouth boss Frank O'Farrell noticed that goalkeeper Billy Bly was missing. A search party eventually found Bly – pacing anxiously in his goalmouth, unaware that the game had been brought to a premature end. When asked how he didn't notice, Bly replied: 'I thought we were putting Preston under a lot of pressure at the other end.'

— ROCK BOTTOM —

In the 1950s the FA Cup belonged to Newcastle, with the Magpies chalking up a hat-trick of final victories in five seasons. Their most comprehensive win was in 1955 when they beat Manchester City 3–1 – but it could have been a very different story that year had it not been for the hapless Arthur Bottom.

Bottom was playing inside-right for Third Division York City, who defied the odds to reach the heady heights of the semi-finals. At Hillsborough against Newcastle the minnows played out of their skins and with the score at 1–1 in the dying minutes they had a golden chance to cause a major upset when, with United's defence caught square, the ball was rolled along the six yard box to number eight Bottom.

Arthur had scored eight goals in York's Cup run, and all that was required was a touch to put the ball in the net for his ninth – but his outstretched foot agonisingly failed to make contact.

The match went to a replay, which a relieved Newcastle won comfortably by 2–0. Bottom was distraught, but his displays had brought him to the attention of the Newcastle management, who eventually brought him to Tyneside three years later.

— CHARLES ALCOCK'S SCHOOLDAYS —

Charles Alcock, founder of the FA Cup, got the idea for the format of the competition from the inter-house knockout matches he used to play when he was a schoolboy at Harrow.

— DELIGHT AT THE DEN —

Millwall made footballing history in 1937 when they became the first side from Division Three to make the FA Cup semi-finals. It was no fluke, either. Although they played every round bar the first at The Den, they proved unstoppable by beating Second Division Fulham 2–0, and both Chelsea and Derby of the First Division by 3–0 and 2–1 respectively.

In the quarters, they faced another First Division outfit, Manchester City, who included stars such as Peter Doherty and Eric Brook in their line-up. A crowd of 42,000 squeezed into the compact South London ground and saw Millwall player-manager Dave Mangnall lead from the front by scoring two goals.

Their opponents in the last four were Sunderland, and the tie was played at Leeds Road, home of Huddersfield Town. On this occasion, playing away from home proved too much for the Lions, but they could be satisfied in the knowledge that they were beaten by the team who would eventually go on to lift the Cup at Wembley.

— WE WOZ ROBBED —

Tottenham Hotspur's 1901 Cup final win remains the only one by a non-League side since the inception of the Football League in 1888, and was achieved courtesy of a 3–1 replay triumph over Sheffield United.

However, Spurs had good cause to believe they had the trophy wrapped up in the first game. They were leading 2–1 with a few minutes remaining when a United break led to a powerful shot which Spurs 'keeper Clawley caught and then fumbled. With the ball dribbling towards the goal line, Clawley dived and managed to push it round the post. The linesman flagged for the corner and the Londoners breathed a sigh of relief. But then the referee, for reasons which even now are unclear, blew his whistle and awarded a goal.

Of course, those were the days when even ludicrously ill-judged decisions were greeted with a sanguine shrug. Spurs had to wait until the following week before making no mistake and lifting the trophy.

— DON'T BET ON WARNER —

Goalkeeper Jimmy Warner was one of the undisputed stars of the Aston Villa team that reached the Cup final against struggling Midlands rivals West Bromwich Albion in 1892, and the main reason the bookies had them at 7–4 favourites to win the trophy for the second time in five years.

However, in the run-up to the big game, 27-year-old Warner started behaving extremely oddly. Not only did he skip training with the rest of the team, but he was spotted on several occasions in conversation with a mysterious man in a sharp suit and hat.

Three minutes into the match, West Brom's Jasper Geddes fired in a long-range shot which Warner caught, but then inexplicably allowed to jump out of his hands and into the back of the net.

Some 20 minutes later, Warner botched a straightforward save to allow West Brom's Nicholls to race in and score the second.

Things got no better in the second half, as 'Baldy' Reynolds of West Brom saw an optimistic punt from 40 yards fly in past the hopelessly out-of-position Warner.

Villa lost 3–0, and almost immediately the inquest began into Warner's lamentable performance. It wasn't long before rumours began to circulate that he had lost a substantial amount of money on a bet and had thrown the Cup final in order to recoup his losses.

Warner denied the accusation, but failed to turn up for Villa's next match. It was said he had run off from the pub he owned with a week's takings and one of the barmaids.

Warner appeared briefly the following season for Newton Heath (who would later become Manchester United), but quickly returned to the shadows where he – and his secret – would remain for the rest of his life.

— RADFORD'S WINNING GOAL —

Ronnie Radford's 30-yard screamer for Hereford against Newcastle United in 1972 was the first FA Cup goal to be voted goal of the season on BBC's *Match of the Day*.

— LUTON'S HOOLIGAN BAN —

Luton Town acted with admirable forcefulness after a pitched battle broke out between their fans and Millwall supporters during a Cup tie in 1985. The directors took the unprecedented step of banning all away supporters from their Kenilworth Road ground, and backed up the decision by threatening to withdraw from both the FA and League Cups if the respective governing bodies tried to force them to change the policy.

Home supporters, meanwhile, were obliged to buy a £1 membership card and sign a good behaviour pledge.

The move did not please the Football League, who took the Hatters at their word and booted them out of the 1986–87 League Cup competition. Fortunately, the FA were in a more conciliatory mood and allowed Luton's membership scheme to continue.

— THE MAN IN WHITE —

Cup final community singing these days involves Charlotte Church, or some other celebrity performer, belting out 'Abide With Me' just before kick-off. But up until the 1970s, a mass-singalong was as much a part of the big day as the match itself.

It was introduced at the 1927 final when conductor T P Ratcliff – known as The Man In White – and the Band of the Grenadier Guards led 100,000 people in spirited renditions of 'Pack Up Your Troubles', 'It's A Long Way To Tipperary', 'All Through The Night' and 'Drink To Me Only With Thine Eyes'.

Ratcliff was followed after World War Two by Arthur Caiger, a London headmaster, and Frank Rae, who continued until the early '70s, when fans decided they would rather chant abuse at each other than sing together.

— THE CUP FINAL KISS OF DEATH —

Four clubs have reached the FA Cup final in a season in which they were relegated and all of them lost at Wembley – Manchester City (1926), Leicester City (1969), Brighton (1983) and Middlesbrough (1997).

— THE CUP FINAL ON THE SPOT —

Once the decision was made to scrap Cup final replays, it was only a matter of time before domestic football's greatest showpiece was decided by the lottery of penalties. Sure enough, after holding out for 120 minutes against Manchester United in the one-sided 2005 final at Cardiff, Arsene Wenger's Arsenal duly won the shoot-out and with it the Cup.

For the record, the shoot-out unfolded like this:

Van Nistelrooy GOAL
1–0 Manchester United

Lauren GOAL
1–1

Scholes SAVED
1–1

Ljungberg GOAL
2–1 Arsenal

Ronaldo GOAL
2–2

Van Persie GOAL
3–2 Arsenal

Rooney GOAL
3–3

Cole GOAL
4–3 Arsenal

Keane GOAL
4–4

Vieira GOAL
5–4 Arsenal

— THE INVINCIBLES —

When Preston North End beat Wolves 3–0 in the 1889
FA Cup final they became the first side to complete the
hallowed League and FA Cup double. Mind you, they
were red-hot favourites: they had already won the
inaugural Football League Championship without
losing a match, and arrived at Kennington Oval for the
final having not conceded a single goal en route.

— SPURS ENTER THE VALE OF TEARS —

Ever since their League and FA Cup double glory of 1961, Tottenham
Hotspur had been football's perennial under-achievers. Long years of
League failure were punctuated by occasional FA Cup final wins, but in
1988 even this reliable silverware supply deserted them.

The circumstances could not have been more humiliating. Port Vale were
a middling Division Three side who had reached the fourth round thanks
to a late winner against non-League Macclesfield. Spurs, managed by
Terry Venables, strolled into town confident that their own faltering
season would soon be resurrected by a comfortable passage to round five.

How wrong they were. The Londoners played so badly that they were
flattered by Vale's 2–1 win.

Ray Walker, a £12,000 signing from Aston Villa, opened the scoring
after 12 minutes with a spectacular 25-yard thunderbolt. A little later
Walker was again involved as Phil Sproson waltzed through lettuce-limp
tackling to make it two.

It was indicative of Tottenham's plight that despite fielding players the
calibre of Chris Waddle, their only goal was scored by centre-half Neil
'Razor' Ruddock in the 64th minute. It was one of the few moments of
anxiety for Vale in a game which they dominated and won at a canter.

— EXTRA PUNISHMENT —

As if being the first player to be sent off in an FA Cup final were
not enough, Manchester United's Kevin Moran faced the further
indignity of not being allowed to collect his winner's medal at the
end of the match. Instead it was posted to him seven weeks later.

— ENGLISH ONLY —

The West Ham team which beat Fulham 2–0 in the 1975 Cup final was
the last to feature an all-English line-up.

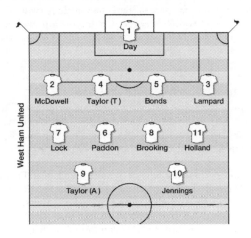

— POETIC VICTORY —

When Tottenham won their first FA Cup in 1901, it inspired the
following piece of flowery verse, which became hugely popular among
the faithful at White Hart Lane.

> *In the Games Olympian*
> *There were heroes, there were men*
> *As we learn in classics lay –*
> *Not more brave than you today,*
> *Not more worthy of renown*
> *Not more fit to wear the crown,*
> *Hands of fair ones in their bowers,*
> *Made for them with Myrtle flowers,*
> *Winners of the Cup at last,*
> *Like those heroes of the past,*
> *Ringing, hearty, bonnie Spurs!*

Well it beats 'You're gonna get your f****** head kicked in!'

— CANARIES SING LOUDEST —

It was 21 years since Herbert Chapman's great Arsenal side had been humbled by Walsall in the third round. Surely, as the Gunners ran out at Highbury against Third Division Norwich City in the fourth round of the 1954 tournament, the unthinkable could not happen again?

Initially, the omens did not look good for giant-killing. Barely two minutes had gone when Arsenal conceded a penalty, but when Bobby Brennan stepped up Jack Kelsey saved the spot-kick easily. In the second half, the Gunners took the lead through Jimmy Logie and the possibilities of a fairytale seemed even more remote.

Enter Tom Johnston, a centre-forward who had been languishing for most of the season in Norwich's reserves. Capitalising on some uncharacteristically lax Arsenal defending, Johnston stunned Highbury by scoring twice in rapid succession.

Suddenly Arsenal were a goal behind with ten minutes remaining, and despite throwing everything at the visitors they were unable to claw back an equaliser. Norwich were through, and the sound in the marble halls of Highbury was of the great Chapman spinning in his grave.

— WINNERS AND LOSERS —

Charlton Athletic played in the 1946 Cup final despite having lost earlier in the competition. Fulham had beaten them 2–1 in the second leg of their third-round tie but Charlton went through on aggregate.

— FA CUP ALL-ROUNDER —

Largely because of their privileged public school backgrounds, many of the early FA Cup stars excelled at more than just soccer. Alfred Lyttelton, who played alongside his brother Edward for Old Etonians in the 1876 final, was an England cricket international – he would become president of the MCC – and English champion at real tennis. He also had an adoring wife, Edith, who wrote of his football: 'He was over six foot one, and his onrush was like a tornado . . . when things grew to be exciting his ardour waxed to a formidable heat, and he would come thundering down with the heavy knees far advanced and all the paraphernalia of a Homeric onset!'

— LAST OF THE GANG —

When Wimbledon beat Liverpool in the 1988 Cup final, they became the 42nd and last different club (at the time of writing) to win the Cup. The Dons had only joined the Football League 11 years earlier. Ironically AFC Wimbledon, the team formed when the old Wimbledon relocated to Milton Keynes as MK Dons in 2003, were accepted into the FA Cup for the first time in 2004.

— HOW IT ALL BEGAN —

'The scene was a small, oak-panelled room at *The Sportsman* office. There sat seven men, dressed in the height of fashion as befitted their place in society. The talk was of the events of the day – the siege of Paris by the troops from Versailles; the proposal before Parliament to abolish the system of purchasing commissions in the Army; the serious illness of Edward, Prince of Wales; the decision of King William of Prussia to assume the title of German Emperor. Soon their conversation drifted to the exploits of their football clubs, for each was a member of one or other of the best-known teams of that period. After the formal business had been dealt with C W Alcock proposed: "That it is desirable that a Challenge Cup should be established in connection with the Association, for which all clubs belonging to the Association should be invited to compete."'
– Geoffrey Green, *The Official History of the FA Cup*.

— THE FIRST BLACK PLAYER —

British football before the war belonged exclusively to white, home-grown players. But after the conflict a number of black performers began to appear, mainly from South Africa. It would be 20 years, however, before one of them played in an FA Cup final. His name was Albert Johanneson, and he had joined Leeds in 1961. An elusive winger, he scored a hatful of goals and helped Leeds to the 1965 final against Liverpool. However, this was the pinnacle of a career which was dogged by racial abuse both on and off the pitch. Regularly called a 'black bastard' by opposing players, Johanneson was also victim of rough-housing and physical intimidation and, despite being a hugely talented footballer, he was never able to fully realise his potential. He died, destitute and raddled with drink and drugs, in 1992, aged 53.

— THE GUNNERS GET SHIRTY —

The 1927 FA Cup final started a tradition at Arsenal which has lasted to this day. Cardiff's 74th-minute winner, scored by Scot Hugh Ferguson, crossed the line after slipping out of the grasp of Arsenal's Welsh goalie Dan Lewis. The Gunners' coach Tom Whittaker believed Lewis failed to hold the ball because of the sheen of his new jersey – and from that day every new goalkeeper's top is softened up in the laundry at Highbury before being worn in a match.

— BEASANT'S PENALTY SAVE —

Cometh the hour, cometh the man. Trailing by a goal to nil against 33–1 outsiders Wimbledon in the 1988 Cup final, Liverpool mounted constant pressure and earned a second-half penalty. As he stepped up to take the kick, Reds striker John Aldridge had history on his side: no-one had missed a penalty in a Wembley final and he had been successful with his previous 11 spot-kicks.

But nobody, it seemed, had told Wimbledon keeper Dave Beasant this. Diving to his left, Beasant flung his 6ft 6in frame at the ball and parried it away, to the disbelief of Aldridge and the majority of the 98,000 crowd.

Beasant's reward for being the first man to save a Cup final penalty was to become the first goalkeeper to receive the Cup itself, when it was presented to him at the final whistle.

— THE 'LUCKY' DRESSING ROOM —

Traditionally Wembley finalists were allocated dressing rooms on an alphabetical basis, with the first-lettered team always going in the North dressing room (except in 1964, when Preston and West Ham were mistakenly allocated the wrong rooms). The South dressing room was always considered the luckier as 70 per cent of winners since the war emerged from it, including giant-killers Sunderland, Southampton, West Ham United and Wimbledon.

— RECORD FA CUP FINAL WINS —

Talk about your name being on the Cup! Here is a list of the FA Cup's most one-sided finals:

1890: Blackburn Rovers 6, Sheffield Wednesday 1
1900: Bury 4, Southampton 0
1903: Bury 6, Derby County 0
1983: Manchester United 4, Brighton & Hove Albion 0 (replay)
1994: Manchester United 4, Chelsea 0

— THE SEVEN-GOAL LOSER —

November 1922, and on the face of it the fourth qualifying round replay tie between Dulwich Hamlet and St Albans had little going for it.

That was before St Albans marksman Wilfred Minter set the match alight with seven goals. Minter got his first hat-trick in 30 minutes, and continued his scoring spree in the second half with three more strikes. If only his goalkeeper had been on form, it might have been a match-winning performance. But Alf Fearn was a centre-half who had stepped into the breach between the posts at the last minute due to an injury crisis. Consequently, Dulwich had as much ease in scoring as Minter – and at full time the score was 6–6.

After ten minutes of extra time, Dulwich made it 7–6 – but Minter was on a roll. With just four minutes left, he flung himself at a corner and headed the ball into the net for his – and St Albans' – seventh goal.

After such a sterling effort in the cause of FA Cup glory, one can only imagine how Minter must have felt to see hapless Alf Fearn make a complete hash of a cross and allow Dulwich's Davis to score the winning goal with the last kick of the game.

— FOOT IN MOUTH —

'We should beat Sutton, but it won't be a landslide. Just a thoroughly professional performance.'
– Coventry City goalkeeper Steve Ogrizovic prior to his side's ignominious third-round exit at the hands of non-League Sutton United in 1989.

— FA CUP TIMELINE —

- **1863**: The Football Association is formed from 12 football clubs in and around the London area.

- **1871**: FA secretary Charles Alcock proposes a knockout cup competition for associated member teams. Four months later, 15 teams have entered and the first FA Cup ties are played.

- **1872**: Wanderers win the first FA Cup by beating Royal Engineers 1–0 at Kennington Oval. The match is watched by 2,000 spectators paying a shilling (5p) each.

- **1873**: Wanderers win their second final. Because the nature of the competition means that teams must battle each other for the right to face the Cup holders, Wanderers don't even play a qualifying game.

- **1874**: The 'challenge' format is scrapped.

- **1883**: The Cup goes north for the first time as Blackburn Olympic beat Old Etonians.

- **1887**: Preston North End beat Hyde by a record score of 26–0.

- **1888**: To prevent one-sided hammerings, the FA introduce qualifying rounds to sort the wheat from the chaff.

- **1895**: The original FA Cup is stolen from a shoemaker's shop in Birmingham. It is never recovered.

- **1915**: With World War One a year old, the FA decide it might be politic to suspend the competition for the duration of hostilities.

- **1919**: The FA Cup resumes.

- **1923**: Wembley Stadium hosts its first FA Cup final. Although its capacity is 125,000, more than 200,000 fans get into the ground, spilling on to the pitch. The FA announce that future finals will be all-ticket.

- **1925**: Teams in the top two divisions of the Football League are made exempt from the qualifying stages and the first two rounds of the Cup.

- **1927**: The Cup final is broadcast live on radio for the first time.

- **1935**: The Cup draw is broadcast live on radio.

- **1938**: The first televised final is watched by 10,000 viewers.

- **1939**: For the second time, the FA Cup is suspended because of war. There are complaints from some quarters that Cup matches should be played because they raise the spirit of the nation.

- **1945**: The Cup resumes, and to kick-start it back to life matches before the semi-finals are played on a home-and-away basis over two legs. If the teams are level after two meetings, they keep going until someone scores a goal.

- **1955**: Jackie Milburn of Newcastle scores what is then the fastest goal in a Wembley final, a bullet header after 45 seconds against Manchester City.

- **1961**: Spurs become the first team during the 20th century to win the League and FA Cup double.

- **1968**: Substitutes are permitted in a final for the first time.

- **1981**: Spurs and Manchester City contest the 100th FA Cup final.

- **1989**: Tragedy strikes as 95 Liverpool fans are crushed to death at an FA Cup semi-final at Hillsborough.

- **1990**: The FA Cup draw is made live on television.

- **1991**: Spurs and Arsenal contest the first FA Cup semi-final to be played at Wembley.

- **1994**: For the first time in its history the FA Cup is sponsored. It now becomes officially known as The FA Cup sponsored by Littlewoods Pools.

- **1997**: Roberto Di Matteo scores the fastest goal in a Wembley final, a 25-yard thunderbolt against Middlesbrough after 43 seconds.

- **2000**: Wembley hosts its last FA Cup final before being demolished and rebuilt.

- **2001**: The Cup final is played at Cardiff's Millennium Stadium, the first time it has been staged outside London since 1923.

- **2005**: Arsenal beat Manchester United in the FA Cup final's first penalty shoot-out.

— AND BACK TO SQUARE ONE —

The advent of radio coverage in the 1920s brought the excitement of the FA Cup final into millions of homes across Britain. But live commentary was as much a novelty to the broadcasters as it was to the listeners. To help the situation, *Radio Times* produced a handy cut-out-and-keep diagram so that fans could follow the action at home. It consisted of a pitch divided up into numbered squares. As the main commentator described the action, an assistant reeled out in which square that action was taking place.

Square One was where the ball ended up if it was passed back to the goalkeeper – hence the phrase 'Back to Square One' to signify returning to where you started.

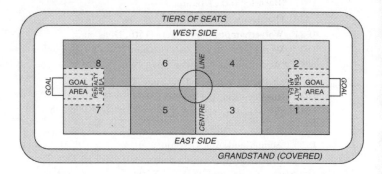

— STIRRING WORDS —

'Cup ties stir the blood of the footballer as no other competition does. When the first half of the season has come and gone and dark December drags its weary way, there is a beacon light ahead that fills the enthusiast with hope and joy. That light is the Cup, and all the glory and glamour that surrounds this wondrous bauble. The heart of the footballer leaps at the name of the Cup. The winter of our discontent is made glorious summer by the dawning of the Cup ties. It is safe to say that no single event in history causes more popular enthusiasm than the simple struggle for the Blue Ribbon of the football world.'
– Alfred Gibson and William Pickford, *Association Football and the Men Who Made It*.

— UNDERDOGS —

The following sides all reached the final of the FA Cup while outside the top division. The asterisks signify those who actually won it.

1890   **The Wednesday** (1st, Football Alliance)

1894   ***Notts County** (3rd, Division 2)

1900   **Southampton** (3rd, Southern League)

1901   ***Tottenham Hostpur** (5th, Southern League)

1902   **Southampton** (3rd, Southern League)

1904   **Bolton Wanderers** (7th, Division 2)

1908   ***Wolverhampton Wanderers** (9th, Division 2)

1910   **Barnsley** (9th, Division 2)

1912   ***Barnsley** (6th, Division 2)

1920   **Huddersfield Town** (2nd, Division 2)

1921   **Wolverhampton Wanderers** (15th, Division 2)

1923   **West Ham United** (2nd, Division 2)

1931   ***West Bromwich Albion** (2nd, Division 2)

1936   **Sheffield United** (3rd, Division 2)

1947   **Burnley** (2nd, Division 2)

1949   **Leicester City** (19th, Division 2)

1964   **Preston North End** (3rd, Division 2)

1973   ***Sunderland** (6th, Division 2)

1975   **Fulham** (9th, Division 2)

1976   ***Southampton** (6th, Division 2)

1980   ***West Ham United** (7th, Division 2)

1982   **Queen's Park Rangers** (5th, Division 2)

1992   **Sunderland** (19th, Division 2)

2004   **Millwall** (15th, Championship)

— A TENSE OCCASION —

The 1934 Cup final between Manchester City and Portsmouth was a cracker, with City coming back from a goal down to score the winning goal with three minutes remaining. But one player was not able to join in the celebrations at the final whistle. Teenage goalkeeper Frank Swift had fainted because of the tension and had to be stretchered off the pitch.

— BOBBY DAZZLER —

'There was no pressure on us because we knew most people outside Ipswich thought it was a foregone conclusion that Arsenal would win. But we knew that we had a plan to win it, and the players to make it work.'
– Ipswich boss Bobby Robson, whose plan for beating Arsenal in the 1978 Cup final was to stifle the Gunners' passing game at source, by man-marking defender Sammy Nelson. The tactic worked a treat. Arsenal were disrupted and Ipswich ran out 1–0 winners against the odds.

— HOT TEMPERS AT ELLAND ROAD —

Police at Elland Road took more than 20 minutes to clear supporters after a crowd invasion near the end of a tetchy FA Cup third-round tie between Leeds and Manchester City in 1978, but the referee refused to abandon the match and Leeds slumped out of the competition 2–1. The fans weren't the only ones who were disgruntled by a sub-standard performance by the home side: at one stage defender Gordon McQueen exchanged blows on the pitch with his goalkeeper David Harvey. McQueen was fined – and responded by slapping in a transfer request. The club, meanwhile, were banned from staging FA Cup ties at Elland Road for three years, a sentence commuted at the end of the season.

— WOULD YOU MIND BEING OFFSIDE? —

On 25 January 1925, the FA took advantage of the fact that a number of top clubs had been knocked out of the Cup in order to experiment with the offside laws. A game was arranged between Arsenal and Chelsea at Highbury, in which a line was drawn 40 yards from each goal, limiting the area in which players could be offside. In the second half, the referee enforced a rule reducing the number of defenders needed between the player of the ball and the goal from three to two. Both proved to be a great success, with only one offside call in the entire game. After a few more experimental matches during the remainder of the season, the two-man plan was adopted by the FA in time for the following term.

— IN THE CUP FOR TOTTINGHAM —

A common complaint about the modern FA Cup is the demise of so many of its traditions – and surely there can be no greater loss than the traditional FA Cup song.

Released in the run-up to the big day in May, these tone-deaf singalongs tended to feature the Cup final squads in V-neck sweaters and casual slacks, looking hugely embarrassed as they mimed along on *Top Of The Pops*.

These were the days before footballers dressed and acted like pop stars – which is why so many fans of a certain vintage remember the music so fondly and why so many of the songs went into the Top Ten.

Arguably the most famous example remains the 1981 Spurs anthem 'Ossie's Dream (Spurs Are On Their Way To Wembley)'. Written by Cockney duo Chas 'n' Dave in honour of Argentinian midfield maestro Osvaldo Ardiles, it contained the immortal lines: 'Ossie's going to Wembley, His knees have gone all trembly', and even featured Ardiles himself rapping the words: 'In the Cup for Totting-ham!'

(Ironically, the game itself will be remembered for the wonder goal scored by Ardiles' fellow countryman Ricky Villa.)

Other FA Cup chart hits include:

- 'Come On You Reds', Manchester United, 1994

- 'Blue Is The Colour', Chelsea, 1972

- 'Anfield Rap (Red Machine In Full Effect)', Liverpool, 1988

- 'Pass And Move (It's The Liverpool Groove)', Liverpool, 1996

- 'Leeds United', Leeds United, 1972

- 'Good Old Arsenal', Arsenal, 1971

- 'Here We Go', Everton, 1985

- 'No-one Can Stop Us Now', Chelsea, 1994

— THE FOSTER'S CUP? —

'The Cup is above sponsorship. It sells itself. The FA is against the whole concept.'

So wrote Ted Croker, FA secretary between 1973 and 1989. In 1987, however, the FA Cup very nearly was sponsored, and from a most unusual source.

Elders was an Australian brewing company whose premium export was Foster's lager. Despite much huffing and puffing about the inviolability of the Cup and the moral consequences of having the world's oldest and most famous domestic knockout competition sponsored by an alcohol manufacturer, the prospect of £20 million over five years was hard to resist.

Indeed the deal might well have gone ahead had Elders not insisted that the FA Cup should be renamed the Foster's Cup.

This was just too much for the traditionalists, who were nevertheless grateful that a sudden crash in the Australian stock market meant that the Elders offer was changed to £10.5 million over four years.

Croker, having been so close to signing the deal, was able to announce that the whole thing was off as the FA had 'insufficient common ground' with its would-be sponsors.

Seven years later, however, Littlewoods Pools offered £20 million plus 'direct support expenditure' – and the FA bit their hand off. So ended 123 years of financial self-sufficiency and the full title of the venerable competition became 'The Football Association Challenge Cup, sponsored by Littlewoods Pools'.

— TV TIMES —

The first televised final was a dour affair between Preston North End and Huddersfield Town in 1938. Other than the presence of the cameras, the game is remembered only for Preston's winning penalty in the last minute of extra time. It was the first time a final had been decided from the spot. Even then it was a scrappy affair, George Mutch putting the ball into the net via the underside of the crossbar.

— STOKOE'S MIRACLE —

'I knew provided we were ready to compete for every ball and not allow Leeds to dominate in midfield we could win. I ran the length of the pitch at the end to congratulate Monty [goalkeeper Jim Montgomery] on his miraculous saves of the second half. I suppose the whole thing was miraculous, really.'

– Sunderland manager Bob Stokoe after his side's astonishing 1–0 FA Cup final win over Leeds in 1973.

— NO PENALTY —

For the first 20 years of its existence, there were no penalties in the FA Cup. The reason for this was simple: the concept had not been invented. The consequences were often chaotic and hugely unfair. In 1891, Stoke were trailing 1–0 to Notts County in the quarter-final when one of their players rounded the 'keeper and fired towards goal – only for one of the County defenders to punch it away with his fist. No goal, and no penalty either – and no semi-final for Stoke, who lost the game.

Even when penalties were brought in shortly afterwards, amateurs objected, claiming that the very idea of a penalty law implied a slur on their morals and might even encourage unsportsmanlike behaviour.

One team, the Corinthians, insisted that their goalkeeper stood by a goalpost while the penalty was taken against them.

— THREE IN A ROW —

With their 2–0 replay win over West Bromwich Albion in 1886, Blackburn Rovers became the first team since Wanderers to win the Cup on three successive occasions. They were awarded a special medal by the FA in respect of the hat-trick – which, nearly 120 years later, they remain the last club to complete.

— IRISH ENTRANTS —

Three Irish teams have played in the FA Cup: Linfield Athletic, Cliftonville and Distillery, a team formed by Belfast whiskey producers.

— GIANT-KILLING: THE TRUTH —

An act of gravity-defying giant-killing is always one of the highlights of the FA Cup, but in reality such upsets are few and far between. Indeed since 1945, top-flight teams have been knocked out by non-League opposition on only four occasions:

1949: Yeovil 2, Sunderland 1 (fourth round)
1971: Hereford 2, Newcastle 1 (third round replay, aet)
1975: Burnley 0, Wimbledon 1 (third round)
1989: Sutton United 2, Coventry City 1 (third round)

Each winner lost in the subsequent round, Yeovil 8–0 at Manchester United, Hereford 3–1 at West Ham in a replay, Wimbledon 1–0 to Leeds United in a replay and Sutton 8–0 to Norwich.

Fifth-round appearances by non-League sides are equally rare:

1948: Blackpool 5, Colchester 0
1949: Manchester United 8, Yeovil 0
1978: Wrexham 1, Blyth Spartans 1
1978: Blyth Spartans 1, Wrexham 2
1985: Everton 3, Telford United 0
1994: Kidderminster 0, West Ham 1

Although not a victory over a top division club, Worcester City's 2–1 triumph over Liverpool in 1959, when the Merseysiders were leading the Second Division, deserves almost equal acclaim.

— BLOODIED BUT UNBOWED —

There have been many blood-and-thunder Cup ties, but none as bloody as the 1978 semi-final between West Bromwich Albion and Ipswich. Having already been involved in a collision which left Ipswich's Brian Talbot concussed, West Brom defender John Wile was then in a clash of heads which left gore streaming down his face. With his side trailing, Wile refused to come off and played the rest of the game with his head swathed in bandages and his shirt covered in blood. It was all in vain, however, as Talbot, Mick Mills and John Wark all scored to propel the East Anglian side to the final with a 3–1 win.

— IN THE BEGINNING —

There were just 15 entrants to the first FA Challenge Cup competition in 1871–72. Only two, Crystal Palace and Queen's Park, are still in existence today. The pioneers were:

Barnes
Civil Service
Crystal Palace
Clapham Rovers
Donnington School (Spalding, Lincs)
Hampstead Heath
Harrow Chequers
Hitchin
Maidenhead
Marlow
Queen's Park (Glasgow)
Reigate Priory

— GOAL-SCORING SPREADSHEET —

FA Cup final result	The last time the score occurred
0–0	2005, Arsenal v Manchester United (Arsenal won on penalties)
1–0	2003, Arsenal v Southampton
1–1	1993, Arsenal v Sheffield Wednesday
2–0	2002, Arsenal v Chelsea
2–1	2001, Liverpool v Arsenal
2–2	1983, Manchester United v Brighton
3–0	2004, Manchester United v Millwall
3–1	1986, Liverpool v Everton
3–2	1989, Liverpool v Everton
3–3	1990, Manchester United v Crystal Palace
4–0	1994, Manchester United v Chelsea
4–1	1946, Derby County v Charlton Athletic
4–2	1948, Manchester United v Blackpool
4–3	1953, Blackpool v Bolton Wanderers
6–0	1903, Bury v Derby County
6–1	1890, Blackburn Rovers v Sheffield Wednesday

— JIMMY'S DANCING SHOES —

As a player for Liverpool in the 1960s Jimmy Melia didn't often fire the public imagination, not beyond Merseyside, at least. But it was a different story in 1983 when, as a football manager, he led Brighton to the FA Cup final.

Although they were struggling in the League – and were relegated two weeks before the final against Manchester United – in the Cup they were a different proposition, knocking out Newcastle United, Manchester City, Liverpool, Norwich City and Sheffield Wednesday.

Although players like Steve Foster and Michael Robinson became household names, Melia was the undisputed star of the show, with his Scouse wit, lived-in face, and especially his white disco-dancing shoes, which he wore for luck in the third round and continued to wear all the way to Wembley.

And he was almost dancing for joy as Brighton took Manchester United all the way in the final, drawing 2–2 before finally going down 4–0 in the replay.

Melia and his shoes did not last long at the Goldstone Ground after the Cup run, but the memory is unforgettable. Today the irrepressible Melia coaches youngsters in Dallas, Texas. The shoes, sadly, did not make the journey across the Atlantic.

— FINALISTS WHO HAVE NEVER WON THE FA CUP —

Club	No of FA Cup final appearances
Leicester City	4
Queen's Park	2
Birmingham City	2
Bristol City	1
Luton Town	1
Fulham	1
Queen's Park Rangers	1
Brighton	1
Watford	1
Crystal Palace	1
Middlesbrough	1
Millwall	1

— GUNNERS SPIKED BY WALSALL —

As Cup shocks go, they don't come much bigger than Arsenal's humiliation at the hands of Walsall in the third round of 1933. Herbert Chapman's men might have been struggling with injuries and indifferent form, but you can only beat what's put in front of you and the side from Division Three (North) grabbed their opportunity with both hands.

Arsenal went into the game on the back of three defeats in five games, and with three of their best players – Eddie Hapgood, Jack Lambert and Bob John – suffering from flu. Still, their side contained the mercurial Alex James and, in Chapman, they had one of the most progressive managers in the game.

It should have been a walk-over, despite Walsall's home advantage. But on the day the Gunners were simply dreadful. Centre-forward Charlie Walsh, one of three new faces, had a nightmare, missing a hatful of chances in an era when tactical substitutes were not allowed. In defence, newcomers Billy Warnes and Tommy Black were even worse, and were badly at fault when Walsall's Gilbert Alsop ghosted into the penalty area and headed home unchallenged from a corner on the hour.

For Black a bad day at the office was compounded five minutes later when he flattened Alsop in the penalty area with a blatant body-check. Bill Sheppard converted the spot-kick for 2–0 and Black, while lucky not to be sent off, got his come-uppance after the game when Chapman immediately put him on the transfer list for conduct unbecoming an Arsenal player.

After his side's stunning 2–0 defeat, the venerated Gunners boss might have considered putting the whole squad up for sale. Sadly, it would be a defeat Chapman would not see avenged. In January the following year, he died after catching pneumonia while watching a third-team match at Guildford. He was replaced by George Allison, who had commentated on the first radio broadcast of an FA Cup final.

— SIGN HERE, PLEASE —

Despite beating Hyde 26–0 in an FA Cup tie in 1887 – still the record margin in the competition's history – Preston North End's players were so impressed by the gallant performance of their opponents' goalkeeper that they asked for his autograph at the end of the match.

— WHITE COLLAR v BLUE COLLAR —

The 1883 Cup final pitched the well-to-do ex-public schoolboys of Old Etonians against working class Blackburn Olympic, who included three weavers, a cotton worker, an iron worker, a picture framer, a plumber and a dentist's assistant in their line-up. In a landmark game the toffs were beaten and the Cup went north of Watford for the first time.

— THE DOC TAKES HIS MEDICINE —

In 1976 the four semi-finalists were Manchester United and Derby County of the First Division, Southampton of Division Two and Crystal Palace of Division Three. When United were drawn against Derby, Reds boss Tommy Docherty announced: 'This is the first time the FA Cup final will be played at Hillsborough. The other semi-final is a bit of a joke, really.'

As if to tempt fate further, when United and Southampton won through to the final, United's winger Gordon Hill said, 'Who are Southampton?'

Needless to say, both he and Docherty were left to eat their words as the Saints marched off with the trophy, thanks to Bobby Stokes's dramatic late winner.

— SHANKS FOR THE MEMORY —

'It was a wet day, raining and splashing, and my shoes and pants were covered in white from the chalk of the pitch as I walked up to the end of the ground where our supporters were massed. We had beaten Leeds United and our players had the arena, but I took off my coat and went to our fans because they had got the Cup for the first time. Grown men were crying and it was the greatest feeling any human being could have to see what we had done. There have been many proud moments. Wonderful, fantastic moments. But that was the greatest day.'
– Bill Shankly on Liverpool's first FA Cup triumph in 1965, from *Shankly* (1976).

— GIGGS' WONDER GOAL —

Manchester United's historic treble in 1999 was no cakewalk. The dramatic last-gasp European Cup win is rightly remembered as the pinnacle, but it should not be forgotten that it took an equally dramatic late winner in the semi-final of the FA Cup to keep the United bandwagon on the road.

With the scores 1–1 in the replay against Arsenal, Ryan Giggs had four world-class defenders ahead of him when he collected possession inside his own half in the 109th minute. following a wayward pass from Patrick Vieira. Giggs seemed to beat each Arsenal man twice at least, as he swayed left to right, right to left and then back and forth once more to leave Vieira, Lee Dixon, Martin Keown, and, finally, Tony Adams in his wake. Even then the Welshman still had it all to do from an acute angle, left of the posts and seven yards out, against England's number-one 'keeper. But he sized up the task and delivered a rising rocket with the left foot that gave David Seaman no chance whatsoever.

The final would prove significantly easier – a 2–0 win over a poor Newcastle United team at Wembley.

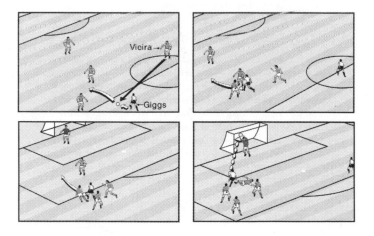

— A DARK DAY FOR DERBY —

Since becoming the first post-war Cup winners in 1946, Derby County had fallen on hard times. In 1955 they were relegated to Division Three (North) for the first time in their history and the following year, a decade since their Wembley glory, they were bundled out of the competition in the most ignominious of circumstances.

Their opponents in the second round were non-League Boston United, and the Baseball Ground watched in disbelief as the part-timers from the Midlands League took the lead after 26 minutes, then proceeded to score two more for a 3–1 half-time lead. After the break things turned from bad to worse as Boston banged home three more in a ten-minute blitz midway through the second half.

The victory had an extra piquancy because seven of Boston's side were former Derby players who had been offloaded following their relegation. One of them, Geoff Hazledine, scored a hat-trick while another, Ray Wilkins, bagged two.

— HOLLYWOOD PLAYER —

Modern footballers are often accused of living like film stars – but even the likes of David Beckham could take a lesson from Sir C Aubrey Smith. Between 1911 and his death in 1948, Smith was one of Hollywood's most prolific movie stars, appearing in 76 films including *Tarzan the Ape Man*, *Lives of a Bengal Lancer*, *Prisoner of Zenda* and *Sixty Glorious Years*.

Before making it big in Tinseltown, however, Aubrey Smith was an equally accomplished sportsman. He played cricket for Surrey and England and, in 1887, he tasted FA Cup fame as a left-winger for the Old Carthusians side which gave Preston North End a fright in the quarter-finals before losing 2–1.

Aubrey Smith was also responsible for introducing cricket to Hollywood, and his club, consisting of expat actors, still plays to this day.

— THE COURAGE OF THE SPARTANS —

The 1977–78 campaign was a good one for non-League clubs, with no fewer than six making it through to the third round of the Cup. Two of them, Blyth Spartans and Enfield, were drawn together, so the disappointment of not landing a lucrative tie against big fish was tempered somewhat by the fact that at least one minnow would progress to the next round.

Indeed, Spartans' 1–0 win left them as the only non-League side remaining in the competition. In the fourth round the pitmen from Northumberland, as they were inevitably categorised in the press, were drawn away to Second Division Stoke where, on a heavy pitch, they staged a magnificent comeback to win the game 3–2.

So it was that Blyth Spartans found themselves in the fifth round, contesting a tie in front of the *Match of the Day* cameras against Wrexham, who had knocked out Newcastle United in the last round.

Few will forget the excitement as Spartans' Terry Johnson pounced on a defensive error to slide the ball through the legs of Wrexham 'keeper Dai Davies early in the game, and how the non-Leaguers then mounted an heroic defence for the remainder of the match as they attempted to become the first side from outside the top four divisions to reach the quarter-finals in modern times.

Then, heartbreak. With less than two minutes remaining, Wrexham were awarded a corner. Over it came, and out came Blyth 'keeper Dave Clarke to catch comfortably. But referee Alf Grey spotted that the ball had been taken from outside the corner quadrant and ordered a retake. Again Clarke leapt to snatch the ball out of the air, but Grey had noticed that the corner flag was not in position and once again ordered a retake.

This time when the ball came over, it was met by Wrexham striker Dixie McNeil, who powered a header past the helpless Clarke and into the net. The replay was staged at Newcastle United's St James's Park, and what a night it was. More than 42,000 supporters crammed on to the terraces, and a further 10,000 were locked outside as the North-East came together to roar the minnows on.

But the miracle was not to be. Wrexham quickly took a 2–0 lead, and extended it to 3–0 late in the second half, Dixie McNeil again playing the role of executioner for the Welshmen.

— THE COURAGE OF THE SPARTANS (CONT'D) —

Terry Johnson's 83rd-minute strike for Spartans brought the house down, however, and secured a place in everyone's hearts for the Northern League minnows who so very nearly pulled off one of the great Cup upsets.

— REVENGE IS SWEET —

Having watched their side being thrashed 9–0 in a League match at Anfield earlier that season, only the most diehard Crystal Palace fan truly expected the Eagles' 1990 FA Cup semi-final against Liverpool to end any differently.

But in a match that will go down as one of the most dramatic of all time, an epic at Villa Park saw the underdogs stun the mighty Reds with an extra-time winner from Alan Pardew.

Liverpool led 1–0 at half-time, thanks to an Ian Rush strike. But an amazing five-goal frenzy in the second half, with hits from Mark Bright, Gary O'Reilly and Andy Gray for Palace and Steve McMahon and John Barnes for the Merseysiders, brought extra time.

The game looked to be heading for a replay until the 109th minute, when Pardew rose to head home past a stranded Bruce Grobbelaar, taking Palace to their first ever Wembley final, against Manchester United.

It was a rare moment of glory for the Eagles, who were threatened with relegation and had taken the field with a number of players injured. In the final itself, they nearly did it again, holding Manchester United to a 3–3 draw with Ian Wright – who had twice broken his leg that season – coming on as a substitute to score two memorable goals.

Oddly subdued in the replay, Palace succumbed to Lee Martin's sole strike.

— FLOWERS OF SCOTLAND —

Rangers, Hearts, Queen's Park and Partick Thistle are existing Scottish League clubs who have taken part in the FA Cup.

— FOOTBALL'S FIRST SUPERSTAR —

With his flowing red beard and white knickerbockers, the Rt. Hon. Arthur Fitzgerald Kinnaird of the Wanderers was no David Beckham – but in the 1870s he was without doubt the most famous footballer of his generation.

He was described by Charles Alcock as 'without exception the best player of the day; capable of taking any place in the field; is very fast and never loses sight of the ball; an excellent captain.'

Kinnaird led Wanderers to victory in the 1873 final, scoring the second goal – the first of nine for Wanderers and Old Etonians, with whom he would win five finals. In 1882 he celebrated the Old Etonians' Cup final victory by standing on his head in front of the Oval pavilion.

His devotion to the game infuriated his wife, Lady Alma Kinnaird, who implored William Kenyon-Slaney, a fellow Wanderer, to convince her husband to stop playing.

'If he goes on,' she said, 'you know it will end in a broken leg, won't it?'

'Yes,' Kenyon-Slaney replied, 'but the leg won't be his own.'

Even when his playing days were over, Kinnaird continued to be involved in football and was FA president for 33 years. Ironically he died in 1923, just four months before the first Wembley Cup final.

— A GOAL-DEN DAY —

There was little cheer for the underdogs in the first round of the 1890–91 competition as the professionals handed out an across-the-board beating to the plucky amateurs. Aston Villa beat the Casuals 13–0, Wednesday put 12 past Halliwell, Nottingham Forest thrashed Clapton 14–0, while newly formed Sheffield United lost 9–1 to eventual finalists Notts County. Kidderminster only lost 3–1 to Darwen, and must have thought they'd got off lightly. But the game was declared void after a protest, and in the rematch Darwen won 13–0.

— NORWICH CITY'S CUP ODYSSEY —

Five years after sensationally dumping Arsenal out of the Cup at Highbury, Norwich City were at it again. In 1959 the Canaries from Division Three reached the semi-final, collecting the scalps of Manchester United (much depleted by the Munich air disaster), Cardiff City and Tottenham Hotspur en route. Throughout they showed tremendous guts, never more so than in the sixth round against Sheffield United, where they earned a replay despite goalkeeper Ken Nethercott being forced to play the last half-hour of the match with a dislocated shoulder.

Their opponents in the semi were Luton Town, but for once that year Norwich's luck ran out. Despite defending doggedly, they went down to the only goal of the game, scored by Irishman Billy Bingham. In the final Luton met an inspired Nottingham Forest side, who won 2–1 at Wembley with ten men.

— MELCHESTER FOR THE CUP! —

Captained by the indefatigable Roy Race, Melchester Rovers have an FA Cup pedigree to rival most other teams, with eight final wins between 1959 and 1990. Roy has scored ten Wembley goals (five more than Ian Rush), and is in the record books for netting the fastest ever Cup goal (four seconds) against Kelburn in 1979. Sadly, his career was cut short by a helicopter crash in 1993.

1959: Melchester 3, Langton United 2 (Race 2)
1961: Melchester 2, Corstone City 1 (Race 2)
1966: Melchester 2, Eastoke United 1 (Race 1)
1970: Melchester 4, Seaford Athletic 1 (Race 1)
1972: Melchester 3, Cranville United 2
1974: Melchester 2, Burndean 0 (Race 2)
1984: Melchester 2, Walford Rovers 1 (Race 1)
1990: Melchester 2, Weston Villa 1 (Race 1)

NOTE: For those too young to remember, Roy Race and Melchester Rovers were the fictional comic-strip heroes who thrilled several generations of readers in the sadly defunct *Tiger*.

— DOING IT THE HARD WAY —

Sheffield United won the Cup in 1899, and few begrudged them their success. To get to the final, the Blades had been drawn away in every round, battled through five replays (including three against Liverpool) and were a goal down to Derby County at half-time in the final. Led by England regular Ernest 'Nudger' Needham and with the legendary William 'Fatty' Foulke in goal, United stormed back with one of the great second-half performances, scoring four unanswered goals and lifting the trophy for the first time.

— EVERTON'S UNUSUAL START —

Everton are one of the giants of the FA Cup, but their initiation into the grand old competition was less than auspicious. In October 1887, the Toffees lost 1–0 at Bolton in the first round. However, Everton lodged an appeal to the FA that Bolton had fielded an unregistered player. The appeal was upheld and the match was ordered to be replayed. The replay was drawn, as was a second replay, until finally, on 19 November, Everton beat the Trotters 2–1 at Anfield.

The controversy was far from over, though. Stung by the reverse, Bolton lodged an appeal of their own, alleging that Everton had paid seven of their registered 'amateur' players. This appeal was also upheld, and Everton were suspended from the competition.

— A NIGHT ON THE TILES —

In the 1960s, England skipper Bobby Moore appeared in an advert extolling the virtue of the good old British pub. But in 1970, when Moore and West Ham team-mates Jimmy Greaves, Brian Dear and Clyde Best decamped to a Blackpool nightclub on the eve of a third-round defeat against the unfancied Seasiders, all four were fined and dropped from the team. Moore was further punished by England boss Sir Alf Ramsey, who axed his talisman from the national squad for the first time since 1962.

— FA CUP FIRSTS —

- **FIRST FA CUP GOAL** – Jarvis Kenrick of Clapham Rovers, 11 November 1871

- **FIRST FA CUP FINAL GOAL** – Morton Peto Betts of Wanderers, 1872

- **FIRST FA CUP FINAL REPLAY** – Royal Engineers v Old Etonians (2–1), 1875

- **FIRST LEAGUE CLUB TO LOSE TO A NON-LEAGUE CLUB** – Stoke (lost 1–2 to Warwick County), 1888–89

- **FIRST SECOND-FLIGHT CLUB TO WIN THE FA CUP** – Notts County (4–1 v Bolton Wanderers), 1894

- **FIRST CUP FINAL PENALTY MISS** – Charlie Wallace of Aston Villa against Sunderland, 1913

- **FIRST EXTRA TIME TO BE PLAYED IN A CUP FINAL** – Aston Villa v Huddersfield Town (1–0), 1920

- **FIRST CUP TIE TO BE DECIDED BY A PENALTY SHOOT-OUT** – the third-place play-off between Birmingham City and Stoke City in 1972. Birmingham won 4–3.

- **FIRST FINAL TO BE DECIDED BY A PENALTY SHOOT-OUT** – Manchester United v Arsenal in 2005. Arsenal won 5–4.

- **FIRST PLAYER TO SCORE IN EVERY ROUND** – Sandy Brown of Tottenham Hotspur, 15 goals, 1900–01

- **FIRST (AND ONLY) NON-LEAGUE CLUB TO WIN THE FA CUP SINCE THE FORMATION OF THE FOOTBALL LEAGUE** – Tottenham Hotspur, 1901

- **FIRST PENALTY GOAL IN FA CUP FINAL** – Albert Shepherd of Newcastle United v Barnsley, 1910

- **FIRST REIGNING MONARCH TO ATTEND AN FA CUP FINAL** – King George V, Burnley v Liverpool, 1914

- **FIRST FA CUP FINAL AT WEMBLEY** – Bolton Wanderers v West Ham United (2–0), 1923

- **FIRST FA CUP FINAL HAT-TRICK** – William Townley of Blackburn Rovers in 6–1 defeat of Sheffield Wednesday, 1890

- **FIRST WEMBLEY GOAL** – David Jack of Bolton Wanderers (two minutes), 1923

- **FIRST ALL-TICKET FINAL** – Newcastle United v Aston Villa (2–0), 1924

- **FIRST (AND ONLY) NON-ENGLISH CLUB TO WIN FA CUP** – Cardiff City (won 1–0 v Arsenal), 1927

- **FIRST RADIO BROADCAST OF FINAL** – Cardiff City v Arsenal, 1927

- **FIRST TIME PLAYERS WORE NUMBERED SHIRTS IN THE FINAL** – Everton v Manchester City, 1933

- **FIRST LIVE TV BROADCAST OF FINAL** – Preston North End v Huddersfield Town, 1938

- **FIRST FLOODLIT FA CUP TIE** – Kidderminster Harriers v Brierley Hill Alliance, 14 September 1955

- **FIRST FA CUP FINAL SUBSTITUTE** – Dennis Clarke of West Bromwich Albion, 1968

- **FIRST FA CUP TIE ON A SUNDAY** – Cambridge United v Oldham Athletic, 6 January 1974

- **FIRST PLAYER SENT OFF IN A FINAL** – Kevin Moran of Manchester United, 1985

— THE BIG SPLIT —

By 1889 entrants for the FA Cup had grown from 15 to 149. As a result the decision was taken to split the competition into two sections: qualifying and proper.

— A PROPER CHARLIE —

With his long hair and untidy appearance, Islington-born Charlie George looked more like a member of Status Quo than an FA Cup hero. Yet it was George who provided the memorable climax to one of the hardest-fought Cup finals of all time when his Arsenal side took on deadly rivals Liverpool in 1971.

It was ten years since North London rivals Spurs had completed the League and FA Cup double, and having won the title a week earlier the Gunners now found themselves on the brink of footballing immortality. Liverpool were in no mood to be generous, however, and after 90 punishing minutes in temperatures of 100 degrees the match was goalless.

It did not remain that way for long. Just two minutes into extra time, dashing winger Steve Heighway's speculative shot caught Arsenal 'keeper Bob Wilson napping and suddenly Liverpool were ahead.

It was a rare blunder which, at such a late stage, might have crippled a lesser team, but Arsenal, led by nuggety Frank McLintock, were made of stronger stuff. Nine minutes later Eddie Kelly became the first substitute to score in a Cup final when he bundled the ball past Ray Clemence.

At 1–1 and with both teams utterly exhausted, the stage was set for Charlie George's *pièce de résistance*. Picking up the ball 25 yards out, George shambled forward and then unleashed a thunderbolt of a shot which flew past the helpless Clemence and into the net.

George did not so much celebrate as collapse on to the turf and await his team-mates to mob him. It was an iconic moment, and summed up Arsenal's never-say-die attitude that took them all the way to their first double.

— A BAZAAR VICTORY —

Bury's 4–0 win over Southampton in the 1900 Cup final was one of the most convincing of all time, yet it very nearly didn't happen. Earlier that year, the skint club had been forced to hold a bazaar, opened by Lord Derby, designed to 'relieve the club from debt and thereby ensure its continuation as an organisation of the first class'.

— A PITCH FIT FOR HORSES —

Wembley Stadium was rightly renowned for its lush green turf, but in 1970 Leeds United and Chelsea could have been forgiven for thinking they were playing on Hackney Marshes. In one of the more bizarre decisions in football history, the Wembley authorities had given the green light to a show-jumping tournament just a few days before the final. Hundreds of hooves and torrential rain conspired to turn the pitch into a sandy quagmire, which had a deleterious effect on the match and was indirectly responsible for the first two goals. First Jack Charlton's header stuck in the sand, evading two defenders on the line, and Leeds were one up. Then Peter Houseman's tame shot rolled instead of bouncing on the treacherous surface, bamboozling 'keeper Gary Sprake for Chelsea's equaliser.

— SUNDAY SOCCER —

The FA Cup made history yet again in January 1974 when, despite complaints from churchgoers, four third-round ties were played on a Sunday for the first time.

— THE ABRAMOVICH OF PRESTON —

Long before Roman Abramovich and his limitless bank account transformed the fortunes of Chelsea, a shrewd football chairman from Lancashire was the first to realise that the quickest way to get the finest team in the country was to buy it.

His name was Major William Sudell, and his team were a little-known outfit called Preston North End. Sudell – who was also the team's manager – went north to Scotland, where he lured top players such as Ross, Drummond and Norton to Lancashire with the promise of lucrative pay-packets and temporary work.

The ploy worked like a dream, and Sudell's Scottish imports formed the nucleus of the team that would win the League and FA Cup in 1889 and go on to become known as 'The Invincibles'.

— THEN AND NOW —

Manchester United superstar Cristiano Ronaldo dominated the 2004 FA Cup final – but would he have been quite so fleet of foot had he been playing for Wanderers in the first Cup final in 1872?

While modern players wear kit made from lightweight synthetic material and boots which are computer-designed, and play with a ball which is made out of aerodynamic plastic, football's pioneers had to make do with rudimentary equipment.

The Wanderers' goal hero Morton Peto Betts wore a heavy cotton shirt, knee-length knickerbockers, thick woollen socks and ankle-high stiff leather boots without studs. The ball was of panelled leather surrounding an inflated pig's bladder, and was virtually impossible to kick once it got wet.

— THERE'S ONLY ONE QUEEN MOTHER —

'It was the centenary Cup final and it is true to say that the Queen Mother received the greatest reception that anybody has ever had at Wembley. When I heard 100,000 rough-and-ready football fans from Manchester and London singing 'There's only one Queen Mother, one Queen Mother' to the tune of one of football's most famous chanting songs, it brought a lump to even a cynical throat like mine.'
– Peter Swales, Manchester City chairman, 1981.

— A NEW HOME —

It may seem hard to believe now, but until the 1920s Wembley was a green, peaceful London suburb complete with a golf course. But in 1921 the FA reached an agreement with the organisers of the British Empire Exhibition to build a 'great national sports ground' in the vicinity, and from that moment, after nearly 50 years, the FA Cup finally had a permanent home.

The Duke of York (later King George VI) cut the first piece of turf on 10 January 1922 and in just 300 days the greatest stadium in the world was built. It was a miraculous piece of engineering, and everything about the reinforced concrete structure was immense: it was 850ft long, 650ft wide and 75ft high, built with 25,000 tons of concrete, 2,000 tons of steel and 500,000 rivets.

Pride of place was taken by its two distinctive domed towers, which soared up to 126ft, and the capacity was a previously unheard-of 127,000.

The timing was perfect: the stadium was completed four days before the meeting of Bolton Wanderers and West Ham United in the 48th Cup final.

— CUP MAXIM —

'There will be no future for the Cup when the impossible is no longer possible.'
– Bryon Butler, broadcaster and writer.

— SOUNESS TAKES HEART —

An FA Cup final is a nerve-wracking affair at the best of times, and it is certainly not the event to be involved in if you've got heart problems. Yet in 1992 Liverpool boss Graeme Souness led his side out at Wembley just weeks after undergoing a triple heart-bypass. Fortunately his side provided few scares as they comfortably beat Sunderland 2–0. Black Cats caretaker boss Malcolm Crosby was also a relieved man, being awarded the job full-time due to the impressive Cup run.

— ALL HALES BREAKS LOOSE —

As Newcastle midfielders Kieron Dyer and Lee Bowyer indulged in their high-profile altercation during a Premiership match against Aston Villa towards the end of 2004–05, seasoned observers were transported back almost exactly 26 years to the day when another pair of so-called team-mates indulged in a bout of fisticuffs on the pitch.

The year was 1979, and in a frustrating FA Cup third-round contest Charlton Athletic of the Second Division found themselves drawing 1–1 with non-League Maidstone United.

Up front for Charlton was the usually productive pairing of Derek Hales and Mike Flanagan. However, that season neither player had been firing on all cylinders and matters came to a head when Hales was ruled offside as he chased a Flanagan through-pass.

Hales complained that the ball should have been played earlier; Flanagan replied to the effect that if Hales wasn't so fat he wouldn't keep getting caught offside.

It is still unclear who swung the first punch, but suddenly both men were scrapping in the middle of the pitch. Referee Brian Martin intervened and sent both players off.

The scores remained level and Charlton won the replay comfortably. Six months later, after playing just one more game for the club, Flanagan was sold to Crystal Palace.

Five years on, however, he was re-signed by Charlton – where he and Hales resumed their strike partnership as if nothing had ever happened.

— WINTER'S TALE —

When the third-round tie between Lincoln and Coventry was called off due to a frostbound pitch, nobody was surprised. After all, in January 1963 Britain was in the icy grip of a severe winter. Quite how severe, however, only became clear when the match was subsequently postponed 15 times. It was eventually played on 7 March.

— DALGLISH IRKED BY STEVENAGE —

Newcastle United's Cup record against non-League opposition was hardly reassuring, so when the Magpies drew Stevenage Borough in the third round in 1998, the vultures began circling the Hertfordshire club's tiny Broadhall Way ground in earnest.

The contrast between the two sides could not have been greater. Newcastle, managed by Kenny Dalglish, cost in the region of £60 million to assemble, £15 million of that having been spent on Alan Shearer.

Stevenage, according to striker Giuliano Grazioli, a mechanic by trade, cost 'three packets of crisps and a Mars bar'.

Dalglish made few friends in the build-up to the game, claiming that it would be a walk-over and that the fixture should be switched to St James's Park, and he must have thought he was right once Shearer gave United the lead after just three minutes.

But on a rutted pitch, against spirited opposition spurred on by the Premiership outfit's perceived arrogance, Stevenage fought back – and with only a few minutes remaining in the first half, Grazioli rose above Steve Watson to plant the ball past Shaka Hislop.

The replay proved that home advantage could be equally treacherous, as United sneaked past to win 2–1 in front of a packed house. Dalglish would eventually lead his side out against Arsenal in the final – but he would not forget his brush with ignominy at the hands of little Stevenage.

— OSBORNE AND OUT —

Roger Osborne was a most unlikely FA Cup hero, and to this day must wish he could remember more about his finest hour.

In 1978 his unfashionable Ipswich Town side found themselves at Wembley against an Arsenal team that contained the likes of Pat Jennings, Liam Brady and Malcolm Macdonald. The Tractor Boys, managed by a comparatively fresh-faced Bobby Robson, were expected to get a thrashing, but in the end the Gunners were lucky to get away with a 1–0 defeat.

After watching his team-mates hit bar and post, and miss a hatful of other chances, the unassuming Osborne finally scored Ipswich's winner after 77 minutes, when he turned home the ball from just inside the penalty area.

He was immediately buried under a pile of jubilant team-mates, and this, combined with the excitement and the 100-degree pitchside heat, caused him to faint.

Osborne was immediately substituted by Mick Lambert – his moment of Cup glory little more than a hazy memory.

— THE WRONG-FOOT GOAL —

Despite his best efforts, Malcolm Macdonald enjoyed zero Cup success as a player. His visits to Wembley with Newcastle United and Arsenal in the finals of 1974 and 1978 both ended in defeat, as did a League Cup final against Manchester City in 1976. But Supermac at least scored one of the most memorable goals of any Cup competition that year against Bolton. Receiving the ball from a throw-in with his back to goal, Macdonald swivelled at the left angle of the box and hit an unstoppable shot into the top corner of the net. The wonder-goal was made even more remarkable by the fact that Macdonald struck it with his 'wrong' right foot.

— STRETCHED STRETCHER-BEARERS —

While playing in an FA Cup quarter-final for Sheffield United in 1899, 22st goalkeeper William 'Fatty' Foulke pulled off a remarkable save and damaged a thigh muscle in the process. He was far too big to fit on any of the stretchers and was eventually dragged off the pitch by six of the heftiest men in the crowd.

— SHOT DOWN —

In 1992, 13 years before they became the first side to lose an FA Cup final in a penalty shoot-out, Manchester United earned the dubious distinction of becoming the first Division One side in the history of the FA Cup to be knocked out of the competition on spot-kicks. Their opponents were struggling Southampton and, having been held to a goalless draw at the Dell, United were confident of progressing.

Things quickly started to unravel, however, as Southampton silenced Old Trafford with goals from Stuart Gray and Alan Shearer inside the first 21 minutes. Andrei Kanchelskis pulled one back just before half-time, but in the second half the Red Devils ran up against a brick wall as the Saints closed ranks at the back. The match was one minute into added time when Brian McClair scrambled a crucial equaliser to take the match into extra time.

Suddenly United were on top, and appeared to have scored when skipper Bryan Robson headed goalwards from close range. The ball was hooked away by Southampton 'keeper Tim Flowers, but despite the fact that TV replays showed the ball was clearly over the line, the referee waved play on.

So penalties it was – and in a tense shoot-out United's internationals Neil Webb and Ryan Giggs both failed to score. Southampton comfortably converted four and were through without having to call upon their penalty expert, Matt Le Tissier.

Flowers, who had performed heroics by saving Webb's penalty, celebrated with a lap of honour that did little to endear him to the Old Trafford faithful.

— SUTTON'S DAY OF GLORY —

Times may have been hard down at Highfield Road in recent years, but in the 1980s Coventry City, under the management of George Curtis and then John Sillett, were a genuine force in English football's top flight. Although they never troubled the upper echelons of the League, the Sky Blues' greatest moment came in the 1987 FA Cup when Keith Houchen's diving header helped beat Tottenham and landed Coventry their first, and to date only, major trophy.

When, two seasons later, they were drawn away to little Sutton United of the Conference, few expected the First Division side to have any trouble in reaching the next stage of the competition – even though the season before Sutton had taken Middlesbrough to a replay.

More than 8,000 spectators packed into Sutton's compact Gander Green Lane ground, and the home side immediately made it clear that they were not overawed by their illustrious opponents. Combining typical grit with a surprisingly smooth passing game, the part-timers more than held their own throughout the early stages. Then, just before the interval, the ground exploded when Tony Rains rose to head home a Micky Stephens corner to put Sutton in front.

In the second half Coventry threw everything at the non-Leaguers and when David Phillips scored it looked as though Sillett's side would come through to win. But in true Cup giant-killing fashion, Sutton battened down the hatches and somehow stopped the First Division side from getting the vital second.

There was a strange inevitability that the goal, when it did come, was scored by Sutton's Matty Hanlan.

Cue scenes of unbridled joy, which goal-scorer Rains remembered well: 'Within 30 seconds of the final whistle the entire pitch was covered with supporters,' he said.

'We didn't want to leave the scene and go back to our changing room. After a while we even went up into the stands to watch the celebrations and soak it all in.

'We all knew we would never have this experience again and we got beaten 8–0 by Norwich in the next round. That result against Coventry was the highlight of my career by a very long way.'

— FAMOUS LAST WORDS —

'I've scored in every round so far and I'm going to get one when we win at Wembley. Say your prayers, Reds. We Geordies are out for glory and we'll get it too. Just wait and see!'
- Newcastle United's Malcolm Macdonald on the eve of their 3–0 Cup final thrashing by Liverpool in 1974.

— AND SMITH MUST SCORE . . . —

BBC Radio commentator Peter Jones' immortal line as Brighton striker Gordon Smith lined up to score a sitter – and the winner – against Manchester United during the 1983 Cup final could only have one outcome. Sure enough, Smith missed. The game finished 2–2, and United comfortably won the replay 4–0.

Smith later recalled his moment of FA Cup infamy:

'Mike Robinson pushed the ball across to me and I took a touch to control it. I wanted to send it in hard and low, first time, but Manchester United's goalkeeper Gary Bailey spread himself well and the ball stuck between his legs. People will say it was an open goal, but how can that be when the 'keeper made a save? If time travel ever becomes a reality, I'll be the first to volunteer. I'll go back and score that goal.'

— BRADY REDEEMED —

'I can now live with the memory of the FA Cup final against Ipswich when I had a nightmare. But I'm not sure how I would have reacted had we not scored that last-minute winner against United. I doubt whether there will ever be a finish to match it.'
- Liam Brady of Arsenal after his side's dramatic 3–2 win over Manchester United in 1979. A year earlier, Brady had been part of a disappointing Gunners side which was beaten 1–0 at Wembley by Ipswich Town.

— CUP C'S —

Five teams beginning with the letter 'C' have won the FA Cup: Cardiff City (1927), Coventry City (1987), Chelsea (1970, 1997, 2000), Charlton Athletic (1947) . . . and Clapham Rovers (1880).

— THE BURNDEN PARK DISASTER —

One of the FA Cup's most unenviable records concerns crowd safety. The Hillsborough disaster of 1989 is still close to everyone's memory, yet more than 40 years earlier there was an eerily similar tragedy across the Pennines in Bolton.

On 9 March 1946 around 65,000 fans crammed into Bolton Wanderers' Burnden Park ground to watch the second leg of the sixth-round tie against Stoke City, with thousands locked out. The game was a huge attraction, not only because Bolton were leading 2–0 but because Stoke boasted the legendary Stanley Matthews in their ranks.

Shortly before kick-off, the catastrophe occurred. Fans outside forced their way in through a broken gate and over a wall, and in the ensuing crush 33 people were killed, with more than 500 injured.

The immediate reaction of the FA was to blame the fans, and it is true that the actions of a few impetuous supporters led directly to so many deaths. But in truth Burnden Park, like most neglected post-war grounds, was a crumbling death trap. With crowds at an all-time high after six years of war, such a disaster could have happened anywhere and at any time.

— SIDE BY SIDE —

In 1930 Huddersfield Town and Arsenal made history when they became the first FA Cup finalists to emerge from the Wembley tunnel side-by-side. This was done as a mark of respect for Gunners manager Herbert Chapman, who had previously been boss of Huddersfield.

— ALL COLOUR —

The 1968 Cup final between Everton and West Bromwich Albion was the first to be televised live in colour. Both teams wore away strips, with Everton rising to the colourful occasion by donning bright amber shirts and blue shorts. But it was West Brom, in all-white kit, who won the Cup with a Jeff Astle goal in extra time.

— VILLA THRILLER —

There was a muddy pitch and the rain came down in stair-rods, but 65,000 people turned up to watch one of the great FA Cup third-round clashes, between Aston Villa and Manchester United at Villa Park in 1948.

Barely 14 seconds had gone when United 'keeper Jack Crompton's first touch was to pick the ball out of the back of his net after Villa's winger George Edwards had blasted home. But if the home crowd thought they were in for an easy day, they were sadly wrong. Incredibly, by half-time United led 5–1.

The architect of a stunning 45 minutes of football was the Red Devils' skipper, Johnny Carey. Undaunted by the disastrous start, he instigated some breathtaking moves and within six minutes United were level through Jack Rowley. As wave after wave of attacks crashed against them, Villa crumbled and Stan Pearson, Jimmy Delaney and Johnny Morris, who struck twice, seemed to have the match wrapped up for Matt Busby's side as they went in for their half-time cuppa.

Whatever was said in the home dressing room did the trick, because in the second half Villa came back with a vengeance. Three goals in rapid succession brought the score to 4–5, and suddenly it was United who were punch-drunk as, roared on by the crowd, Villa strove to nail the equaliser, which nearly materialised as a snap-shot by Trevor Ford rattled the visitors' crossbar.

But with Carey orchestrating affairs, United decided that their only option was to attack and try to kill the game off. Sure enough, they battled their way to the other end of the pitch and won a corner. Charlie Mitten sent the ball sailing across and there was Pearson to fire the ball into goal through a forest of legs.

United were home by the remarkable score of 6–4, and that year they proved unstoppable. They reached the final where they beat Stanley Matthews' Blackpool 4–2.

— PROFESSIONAL STANDARDS —

Blackburn Olympic's 1883 Cup final win over Old Etonians was the first by a northern team and the first by a 'professional' team. Although playing for money would not be legalised for two more years, Blackburn were professional in all but name.

As well as paying their players, and often enticing better ones from as far afield as Scotland, they adopted a far more stringent approach to training than their opponents, to whom training was akin to cheating. On their way to the final, for example, Olympic stopped off for a week at Blackpool, where the footballers were put through their paces on the sands as well as being obliged to take invigorating brine baths.

They also revolutionised the tactics of the game by eschewing the long-established kick-and-rush techniques used by public school boys in favour of smooth long-distance passing between the wings.

In the final, Olympic only won by 2–1 in extra time, but the community of Blackburn never looked back. The following year Blackburn Rovers beat Queen's Park in the final and the Lancashire town was home to the Cup for six of the next nine years.

— A TEAM TO RATE AMONG THE LEGENDS —

'You've got to put this team up there with the best of any era. It has so much talent and ambition and so many good players coming through.'
– Sir Bobby Charlton after watching Manchester United's 1–0 Cup final win over Liverpool in 1996, a result which clinched their second League and FA Cup double.

— ALWAYS ON A SUNDAY —

On the way to winning the FA Cup in 1990, Manchester United played every game until the semi-final replay on a Sunday.

— HEROIC SAVE —

In the days before substitutes, an injury to the goalkeeper was the biggest nightmare faced by any team. In 1959, three years after Bert Trautmann's broken-necked heroics for Manchester City at Wembley, Norwich City made it to the semi-finals, thanks in no small part to the brilliance and bravery of goalkeeper Ken Nethercott. He defied Sheffield United in the quarter-final despite playing with a dislocated right shoulder.

— THE TIE THAT WENT ON AND ON AND ON AND . . . —

On the face of it, the fourth qualifying round tie between non-Leaguers Alvechurch and Oxford City in 1971 had little going for it unless you were one of the couple of hundred spectators who attended the game at Alvechurch's tiny ground.

Six matches, nine goals, five venues and more than nine hours later, the fixture had entered FA Cup folklore as its longest ever tie.

The first match ended in a 2–2 draw, the replay at Oxford 1–1. With hopes high that a neutral ground might secure a result, the second replay took place at St Andrews, home of Birmingham City. When this ended 1–1, the bandwagon moved to Oxford United's HQ, where two goalless matches were played out in front of increasingly incredulous spectators. Finally, the teams trotted out for the fifth replay at Villa Park where Alvechurch won by a single goal to nil.

It was perhaps inevitable that, having gone to such lengths to qualify for the first round proper, Alvechurch were duly dumped out of the Cup by Fourth Division Aldershot.

— A LUCKY BREAK? —

When Blackburn's Dave Whelan broke his leg during the 1960 Cup final against Wolves, the injury was so severe that it ended his top-flight career. But some breaks are better than others, perhaps concentrating the mind on other priorities, and Whelan later set up JJB Sports, the nationwide chain that would eventually make him a millionaire several times over.

— A SWIFT DISMISSAL —

One of the many teams to appear briefly in the FA Cup in its early years before being lost in the mists of oblivion were the Swifts, who hailed from Kensington. Almost nothing is known about them now except for the one incident in 1888 which raised them into the realms of Cup trivia.

In the fourth round the Swifts were drawn against Crewe Alexandra, who had already dismissed Druids and Northwich Victoria and were firmly expected to progress without difficulty.

The game, however, finished 2–2 – a result which was so unexpected that Crewe's officials decided some sort of skulduggery must be afoot. Sure enough, a detailed post-match investigation revealed that one crossbar was two inches lower than the other and two inches below the height required by the rules.

The Swifts were duly disqualified from the competition and Crewe proceeded to the semi-finals, where it wasn't the crossbar that scuppered them, but 'The Invincibles' of Preston North End, who won 4–0.

— THE LUCK OF THE DRAW —

'To succeed in the Cup you want luck, a deal of it, not so much on the field as in the council chamber where ties are fortuitously arranged. There are times, especially when it goes against you, when you are inclined to believe that too much luck enters the tournament. Personally, however, I would not have the conditions altered. Indeed, to tinker with them would rob the event of much of its fascination.'
– Herbert Chapman, Arsenal manager.

— COSMOPOLITAN FOREST —

Nottingham Forest are the only side to have played FA Cup ties in England, Scotland, Ireland and Wales.

— FAIRY-TALE STOREY —

In 1971 Arsenal won the League and FA Cup double for the first time, and Charlie George's spectacular Wembley winner against Liverpool remains indelibly linked to their achievement. What tends to be forgotten, however, is just how close the Gunners came to crashing out of the competition in the semi-final.

Indeed, had it not been for goals from a most unexpected source, Stoke City would have been on their way to Wembley.

Peter Storey was a no-nonsense midfield stopper who rarely ventured far enough forward to trouble the opposition goalkeeper. But that day he scored two – and even had a hand in one of Stoke's goals.

Storey's eventful match got off to a disastrous start when his attempted clearance smashed off Denis Smith and rocketed into the net past a stranded Bob Wilson in the Arsenal goal. Things got even worse for the Gunners before half-time when John Ritchie broke clear and doubled the lead for the men from the Potteries.

With Charlie George misfiring up front, Storey took it upon himself to push forward. He was rewarded soon after the interval when a half-cleared ball came to him on the edge of the box and he hammered an unstoppable volley past Gordon Banks.

With the game drifting into stoppage time, Arsenal won a corner. Frank McLintock's header was goalbound when Stoke's John Mahoney leapt across and palmed the ball off the line. It was a penalty – but the Gunners' regular spot-kick expert George had been substituted. Up stepped Storey and, with the last kick of the match, he coolly sent Banks the wrong way to earn his side a barely deserved replay.

The rest, as they say, is history.

— A CUP OF PLENTY —

With 661 applicants, the 2004–05 FA Cup was the biggest ever and contained a number of sides who had never taken part in the grand old competition before. They were:

AFC Wimbledon
Almondsbury Town
Alsager Town
Barkingside
Bishop's Cleeve
Bodmin Town
Broadbridge Heath
Cammell Laird
Coalville Town
Cornard United
Eton Manor
Felixstowe & Walton United
Frimley Green
Godmanchester Rovers
Hamworthy United
Kennek Ryhope CA
Leiston
Leverstock Green
Long Melford
March Town United
Mile Oak
Newcastle Benfield Saints
Newport Pagnell Town
North Greenford United
North Shields
Padiham
Potton United
Retford United
Rye & Iden United
Saltash United
Silsden
Steyning Town

Wantage Town
Westfield
Woodford United
Wootton Bassett Town

In all there were 782 games and 2,528 goals (including the nine penalties in the final). A total of 2,161,406 spectators watched the tournament, in which there were 48 hat-tricks, including five four-goal hauls and three players scoring five.

— SHERRY AND EGGS —

With odds of 5,000–1 against them, Yeovil Town of the Southern League were not expected to create waves in the 1948–49 FA Cup. Yet that year the unfancied West Countrymen not only reached the third round, but then proceeded to beat Second Division Bury. In the fourth round they were up against mighty Sunderland, known as the 'Bank of England Club', and this time even the most diehard Yeovil fan was expecting a hammering. However, the non-Leaguers had a couple of aces up their sleeves. One was their secret training diet of glucose and sherry, mixed with eggs. The other was their infamous sloping pitch.

Cheered on by a huge crowd standing on terracing made partly from beer crates, and with reporters hunched over desks purloined from a local school, Yeovil took a shock 2–1 lead. With 15 minutes to go, the tactics were simple: the ball was either hoofed to the bottom of the slope, or else out of the ground. At one stage Sunderland's star player, Len Shackleton, pleaded with Yeovil's player-manager Alec Stock: 'Don't spoil a good game.'

In similar style to Bill Shankly 20 years later, Stock replied: 'It's not a good game. It's life and death!'

Yeovil clung on to record a famous victory and earn a fifth-round trip to Old Trafford to meet Manchester United. But while the sherry-and-eggs diet was available, the sloping pitch was not – and United ran out 8–0 winners.

— WEMBLEY'S TWIN TOWERS —

When it was decided to knock down the decrepit old Wembley Stadium and replace it with a new one for the 21st century, the big debate was whether the Twin Towers should be integrated into the new design. After all, even though the 126ft high domes served no useful purpose other than as decorations, they had become the unmistakable symbol of English football for nearly 80 years.

Eventually, despite complaints, the decision was made to demolish the famous landmarks along with the rest of the stadium. However, perhaps out of respect for the end of an era, the Twin Towers were destroyed last, standing proud for one last time as a chapter of history was demolished around them.

— EVERTON'S REPLAY RIOT —

Football, as we all know, is a funny old game. But in 1988 even seasoned terrace observers were left scratching their heads at the vagaries of the form book.

Everton and Sheffield Wednesday were paired in the third round of the Cup, but neither side seemed capable of despatching the killer blow. After the first match ended 1–1, the sides were still locked together after two replays also finished one-apiece.

For the third replay, the action switched to Hillsborough where, after just 20 seconds, Wednesday striker Colin West squandered a golden opportunity to give his side a priceless lead.

It was to be Wednesday's last meaningful contribution to the game. In an astonishing 45 minutes, Everton suddenly found they were able to unlock the Owls' defence at will and scored five unanswered goals. Chief assassin was Graeme Sharp, who rattled in a hat-trick. Adrian Heath and Ian Snodin added the other two to leave Wednesday dead and buried by the interval.

In the second half, it was as if the goal blitz had never happened as both sides reverted to type and failed to trouble the scoreboard operator again.

— POOR OLD PLUMLEY —

You had to feel sorry for Gary Plumley in the spring of 1987. One minute he was working as a part-time waiter in a wine bar, the next he was in goal for Watford in the semi-final of the FA Cup. Plumley was called into action when regular goalkeepers Steve Sherwood and Tony Coton were injured, and it was his misfortune to be the last line of defence against a Tottenham Hotspur side that contained Glenn Hoddle, Chris Waddle and Osvaldo Ardiles in midfield and 49-goal Clive Allen up front.

Within 30 minutes, Spurs were three goals in front and their supporters were taunting poor Plumley with the chant of: 'You should have stayed in your wine bar.'

The match ended 4–1, and Plumley never played for Watford again.

— BRUMMIES UNITED —

The first all-Birmingham final was played in 1887 when 15,500 fans saw Aston Villa beat West Bromwich Albion 2–0 at Kennington Oval. It was a bitter pill for the Baggies to swallow, having been beaten by the same score by Blackburn Rovers the previous year.

— THE BAD LAD OF READING GAOL —

It's 1894 and with a vital qualifying match against Southampton St Mary's looming, non-League Reading are desperate for the services of star striker Jimmy Stewart. Unfortunately Stewart, a soldier, is currently locked up in the guardhouse for unspecified misdemeanours.

Armed with a bottle of whisky, Reading secretary Harold Walker arrives at the gaol and proceeds to get the guard drunk. Once the fellow is well inebriated, Walker persuades him to let Stewart out for the afternoon – and the gaolbird duly scores the winner.

Southampton, understandably, lodge a complaint but it is not upheld. Stewart is a registered Reading player, and there is nothing in the FA rules to say that he can't be a prisoner as well.

— FIRST AND LAST —

The 1892 final between West Bromwich Albion and Aston Villa marked the last time Kennington Oval hosted the gala day of English football, due to safety concerns after more than 25,000 fans packed into the ground.

— LEEDS BLOW THE DOUBLE —

When Allan 'Sniffer' Clarke stooped to head Leeds United's second-half winner in the 1972 Cup final against Arsenal, it set the Tykes up for an historic double. All they had to do was draw with Wolves 48 hours later to clinch the League title. Amazingly, they lost 2–1, handing the title to Derby County by a single point.

— BROADCASTING RIGHTS —

The first of many wrangles between the FA and the broadcasters came in 1929 when, for the first time, the FA demanded payment from the BBC in return for rights to radio commentary for an early-round tie between Bolton and Portsmouth. Agreement could not be reached, and instead listeners had to make do with sporadic reports of the match.

The deadlock continued right up until the final, and with neither side prepared to back down the public was in uproar. There was even a scathing leader column about the issue in *The Times*.

It was left to the Bishop of Buckingham to intervene with an impassioned plea to the FA not to 'deprive the general public, especially the blind, the sick and the infirm' of live running commentary.

The words of the man of God did the trick and on 4 April 1930 more than a million people tuned in to the dulcet tones of George Allison describing Arsenal's 2–0 win over Huddersfield.

— THE MANCHESTER FINAL —

Such was the popularity of the FA Cup that in 1893 London was unable to provide a venue big enough to house the crowd expected to watch the final. Instead, the match between Wolves and Everton was played at Manchester's Fallowfield stadium. More than 45,000 witnessed the action. The following year the venue was switched to Everton's Goodison Park before returning to London in 1895.

— WELSH WIZARDS —

The first Welsh club to take part in the FA Cup were the long-forgotten but imaginatively named Druids of Ruabon. Formed in 1877, they entered the Cup for the first time six years later and reached the fifth round – but had a singular lack of success thereafter. Winners of the Welsh Cup in 1898, the Druids were drubbed by Rock Ferry in the second qualifying round that year and didn't need the runes to tell them the English version was not for them.

— UNITED ARE CHERRY BOMBED —

In the 1980s, Manchester United flattered to deceive. Despite a flamboyant manager in Big Ron Atkinson and stars such as Bryan Robson, Arnold Muhren and Ray Wilkins in their line-up, the Reds consistently under-achieved in the League.

The FA Cup provided them with much-needed silverware in 1983 and 1985, but was also responsible for one of the most ignominious moments in their illustrious history.

It was 1984, and when United, the holders, pitched up at Dean Court for a third-round clash with lowly Bournemouth, not even the most romantic observer gave the Third Division side a cat in hell's chance.

But Bournemouth, coached by one Harry Redknapp, had other ideas. Straight from the first whistle, the Cherries set about the First Division aristocrats like dervishes, utilising the small, rutted pitch to unsettle United's cultured passing game.

Frustrated and outplayed, United began making errors and when Milton Graham scored for Bournemouth the side from Old Trafford were reeling. Ian Thompson's second goal knocked them flat on their backsides in the mud, and by the end of the match the Cherries could have considered themselves unlucky not to have scored three or four.

United weren't the only big-name side to come a cropper that day. Nine First Division sides exited the Cup, including the mighty Liverpool, who were toppled by Brighton.

— LAWS OF THE GAME —

When the laws of football were framed in 1863, it was assumed that because both sides would adhere to them without question there was no need for a referee. This changed with the advent of the FA Cup. Now there were two umpires, one in each half of the field, with a referee observing events from the touchline. If the umpires could not agree upon a decision, they would refer the matter to the referee who would make the definitive ruling.

— THE LLOYD GEORGE OF WELSH FOOTBALL —

In 1904, a decade before Stanley Matthews was born, the man widely regarded as being his footballing predecessor scored the solitary goal which clinched victory for Manchester City in the first all-Lancashire FA Cup final against Bolton.

Like Matthews, Billy Meredith was a right-winger of genius, known variously as 'The Welsh Wizard' and, more imaginatively, 'The Lloyd George of Welsh football'. Also like Matthews, Meredith's career at the top was almost supernaturally extended.

In all, he played for 31 years for Northwich Victoria, Manchester City, Manchester United, Manchester City again, and Wales – that's more than 1,560 games, scoring 470 goals.

Indeed, one of his last games was for Manchester City in an FA Cup semi-final against Newcastle in 1924, when he was four months shy of his 50th birthday.

— A RIVAL IS BORN —

For nearly 90 years the FA Cup had existed in splendid isolation, the first and only Cup competition for English clubs. In 1960, however, it found it had a rival when the Football League decided to launch its own knockout contest. The League Cup differed in that non-League clubs were not included – and initially the competition attracted only lukewarm attention from those allowed to enter. In its first year Arsenal, Sheffield Wednesday, Spurs, West Bromwich Albion and Wolves declined to take part. Although interest eventually picked up, and victory earned a European place, the competition has never succeeded in emerging from the shadow of the FA Cup, and in recent years most of the top teams have chosen to field second-string sides.

— NORTHERN INVADERS —

The first side from outside London to reach the final were Blackburn Rovers, who were beaten 1–0 by Old Etonians in 1882.

— A WEEK TO REMEMBER —

Sunderland superstar Raich Carter never forgot his honeymoon. Married on a Monday, Carter immediately headed south to train with his team-mates in preparation for the 1937 final against Preston North End. On the Saturday he scored in his side's 3–1 win and, as captain, received the FA Cup from the Queen. What his wife thought of it all is not recorded.

— THERE'S NOWT AS QUEER AS FOULKE —

William 'Fatty' Foulke was a colossus who began his goalkeeping career weighing 15 stone and finished it at 22 stone. Still, he combined his enormous size with surprising agility and huge natural talent, which saw him capped for England.

Foulke also had a volatile temper, and on more than one occasion he gave away penalties by picking up opposing strikers and dangling them by their ankles.

He played in three FA Cup finals for Sheffield United, winning two and losing one, and he was particularly incensed following the 1902 encounter with Southampton, which ended in a 1–1 draw. After lying in the bath contemplating the injustice of it all, he got out and went in search of the referee. The circumstance that he was stark naked and the referee was already enjoying post-match hospitality in the boardroom did not bother him.

Indeed, as Foulke once famously said: 'I don't mind what you call me as long as you don't call me late for lunch.'

Fortunately for Foulke – and the ref – Sheffield won the replay 2–1.

— FIRST-CLASS OXFORD —

In 1962 Oxford United were elected to the Football League. Two years later, they stunned the nation by beating Blackburn Rovers 3–1 to become the first side from Division Four to reach the quarter-finals of the FA Cup. Star man for Oxford was one Ron Atkinson, who would later become manager of Manchester United.

— NON-LEAGUE RECORD —

In 1957–58 Hereford United equalled the record score for non-League clubs against League opposition in the FA Cup when they beat Queen's Park Rangers, then of Division Three (South), by six goals to one in the second round.

— THRILLER ON THE TRENT —

The FA Cup quarter-finals of 1967 brought together two sides at the top of their game. Nottingham Forest were chasing the League and FA Cup double, while their opponents that day at the City Ground were Cup holders Everton.

The two high-flyers did not disappoint, providing one of the most thrilling ties of all time.

Both teams were rich in talent, but in Jimmy Husband (Everton) and Ian Storey-Moore (Forest) both possessed a deadly goal-scorer, and one of the highlights of the match was the personal duel that developed between the two of them.

In the end, Husband scored two and Storey-Moore three as Forest scraped a 3–2 win. Storey-Moore's crucial third goal was perhaps the pick of the bunch, simply because of its bizarre nature. His first shot struck a defender; then, picking up the rebound, the England winger blasted his follow-up straight at goalkeeper Rankin, who somehow managed to parry it. Again the Forest man was first to the ball, but this time his shot cannoned back off the crossbar. In the goalmouth melee that followed, it was Storey-Moore who launched himself at the leather, finally putting it in the back of the net at the fourth attempt.

It was a dramatic goal which was a fitting finale to a breathless game. Unfortunately for Forest, they would lose the semi-final to Spurs and be pipped to the League title by Manchester United.

— PROPHETIC WORDS —

'I always play well against Leeds. I always score goals against Jack Charlton.'
– Colchester's Ray Crawford before his side's shock 3–2 Cup win over Leeds in 1971, in which he scored twice.

— PRESTON HUMBLED —

Preston North End were the first team to complete the League and FA Cup double. But on a bitterly cold day in December 1989, those glory days were little more than a distant memory as the Deepdale men, by then operating in the Third Division, were dumped out of the Cup by little Whitley Bay of the Second Division of the HFS Loans League.

Whitley Bay had already beaten Fourth Division Scarborough in the first round and, with the conditions and their own muddy pitch in their favour, they were determined to progress to the heady heights of the third.

The writing was on the wall in the first half when defender Peter Robinson forayed forward and struck a shot which bobbled into the net past Preston 'keeper Alan Kelly. Then the execution was completed in the second period when Kevin Todd – once of Newcastle United – put the final flourish to a sweeping move that left Preston standing like statues in the quagmire.

In the third round, Whitley Bay's glorious Cup run was ended with a 1–0 defeat at the hands of Rotherham.

— LIFE BEFORE ELTON —

When rock star Elton John – born Reginald Dwight – appeared on the pitch before his beloved Watford's FA Cup final against Everton in 1984, it was not the first time a member of his family had caused headlines at Wembley. In 1959 Elton's uncle Roy Dwight scored the opening goal as Nottingham Forest beat Luton Town 2–1. But for Roy, like Elton 25 years later, the game would end in tears, as he was stretchered off with a broken leg after 30 minutes.

— A RECORD UNLIKELY TO BE BEATEN —

The most goals in an FA Cup run was in the 1887–88 season, when Jimmy Ross of Preston North End scored 20 times in eight games.

— NO-NONSENSE TACTICS —

'I told our players before the game that even if the Queen was watching, if there was any danger they should kick the ball into the Thames. It was important that we should not let United settle into any kind of tempo. We were honest enough to admit to ourselves that if we let them play they could tear us apart. Our objective was to stop the ball getting to their danger men, and that meant every man had to work twice as hard as usual to prevent United passes getting through. It was a magnificent team performance, and I'm so pleased for Bobby Stokes (who scored the game's only goal). They'll give him the freedom of Hampshire after this.'

– Southampton boss Lawrie McMenemy reveals the tactics which helped his side to a shock 1–0 win over Manchester United in the 1976 FA Cup final.

— 'TREBLECOCK' AND KAVANAGH —

Mike Trebilcock was a 21-year-old virtual unknown when he was plucked from the reserve team and scored two goals in Everton's dramatic 3–2 Cup final win over Sheffield Wednesday in 1966. In fact he was so unknown, his name wasn't even included in the match programme.

The main talking point about him was his surname which, until the final, was pronounced as it was spelt.

It was commentator Kenneth Wolstenholme who spared the nation's blushes by renaming the youngster 'Tre-bil-co' – a pronunciation which was not used by the opposition fans.

Another Evertonian who tasted national fame that day was supporter Eddie Kavanagh, who was so delighted he ran on to the pitch during the game and, to whoops of delight from the crowd, managed to evade several chasing policemen before being rugby-tackled to the ground in the penalty area.

With his broad grin and his braces, 'Fast Eddie' remains a Wembley legend.

— COLCHESTER SLAY THE GIANTS —

As giant-killings go, they don't come much more memorable than Colchester's astonishing victory over Leeds United in the fifth round in 1971. The two sides were footballing opposites in almost every conceivable way: Leeds were a top-flight super-power with a star-studded squad that included the likes of Billy Bremner, Norman Hunter, Mick Jones and Johnny Giles; Colchester were 75th in the Football League, a ragtag outfit consisting of rejects, free transfers and so many over-thirties that they were known as Grandad's Army.

Yet the FA Cup is a great leveller, and at Colchester's tiny Layer Road ground the superstars from Yorkshire were pummelled into submission by a team who, by rights, should have been blasted out of the competition.

The minnows were two goals up within 25 minutes thanks to 34-year-old former England centre-forward Ray Crawford. They made it three after 55 minutes when Dave Simmons gleefully tapped home past Gary Sprake.

Leeds came storming back with goals from Hunter and Giles, but by then it was too late and Colchester managed to hang on for a victory which is still talked about in that corner of Essex.

— INVASION —

Pitch invasions were very much the vogue in 1978. A third-round tie between Leeds and Manchester City was held up for 20 minutes, while in the quarter-final Millwall fans fought with police for 18 minutes during their side's ignominious 6–1 thrashing at the hands of eventual Cup winners Ipswich. 'These people are killing our game,' Portman Road boss Bobby Robson said later. 'I would turn a flame-thrower on them.'

— BROTHERS IN ARMS —

In 1876 brothers Hubert and Frank Heron turned out for Wanderers in the FA Cup final against Old Etonians – who included brothers Alfred and Edward Lyttelton in their line-up.

— THE SCOTS GO IT ALONE —

In March 1873, a year after Charles Alcock et al had established the English FA Cup, the Scots decided to launch their own knockout competition. However, with a credit balance of just £1.11s.4d (approximately £1.57) in its first year, the Scottish FA had to seek donations from its member clubs to pay for the trophy and badges – which cost £56.12s.11d (£56.64 or thereabouts). The competition also struggled when one of the leading Scottish clubs, Queen's Park of Glasgow, elected to play in the English tournament as well.

— THE REVIE PLAN —

In later years Don Revie would make a name for himself as a successful manager of Leeds and as a less successful England boss. But while playing for Manchester City against Birmingham City in the 1956 Cup final, Revie's tactical nous was put to good use on the pitch as the Sky Blues romped to a 3–1 win.

A late call-up to replace striker Bill Spurdle, who was stricken with an outbreak of boils, Revie was positioned in a highly unorthodox deep-lying position, a tactic which flummoxed the Birmingham defence and allowed him the space to create two of the three Manchester goals for Jack Dyson and Bobby Johnstone.

The match would later become infamous because of goalkeeper Bert Trautmann's broken neck, but at the time it was the revolutionary 'Revie Plan' which captured the imagination and led to a widespread rethink of the rigid tactics and field positions which had dominated football in the modern era.

— TV FAVOURITE —

The 1970 FA Cup final replay between Leeds United and Chelsea attracted a mammoth 28.49 million viewers – making it the second-most-watched television programme of the decade, behind the Apollo 13 splashdown.

— RUSHIE CLINCHES THE RECORD —

Liverpool's 7–0 hammering of Rochdale in the third round of the 1995–96 competition included one strike by revered Merseyside marksman Ian Rush. It was Rush's 42nd FA Cup goal, making him the tournament's leading post-war scorer and beating the old record of Denis Law. Liverpool made the final that year but were pipped 1–0 by an Eric Cantona-inspired Manchester United. Later Rush stretched his record to 43 goals, courtesy of a strike for Newcastle United.

— NO WARM WELCOME FOR MATTHEWS —

A year after winning the hearts of the nation for finally securing an FA Cup winner's medal in the 1953 final, playing for Blackpool against Bolton, Stanley Matthews returned to his native Potteries for a fifth-round tie against Port Vale. But if he was hoping for a hero's welcome, the former Stoke winger was to be sorely disappointed.

The side from Division Three (North) fancied their chances against the First Division outfit, and manager Freddie Steele had a clear plan of action.

Steele had been a team-mate of Matthews in the 1930s, and was all too aware of the sensational strengths of 'The Wizard of Dribble' – and also of his weaknesses. He instructed his men to block Matthews' usual hunting ground on the right wing, forcing him inside and into the cloying mud of the midfield. The ruse worked a treat. Every time Matthews got the ball, he was forced to dig it out of the mire. By the time he had done this, he was surrounded by Vale's uncompromising defence.

With their main outlet nullified, Blackpool stuttered. Vale needed no second invitation to go for the kill, and ran out 2–0 winners.

It was to prove a good run for the Staffordshire side. In the next round they beat Orient 1–0, and only narrowly lost to eventual Cup winners West Bromwich Albion in the semis.

— IN MEMORIAM —

At the start of the 20th century a highly popular means of rubbing salt into losers' wounds were the so-called 'Football Funeral Cards'. These were printed in local newspapers in the 'in memoriam' section and could often be scabrously funny.

When Everton were knocked out of the Cup by Wolves one year, the Midlanders immediately posted a card in memory of 'Everton Football Team – who departed from the Cup competition through a severe attack of Wolves, and whose hopes were interred at the Football Cemetery the next day.'

The accompanying poem must have made painful reading to any true blue Merseysider:

> *They came in all their glory,*
> *From that noted Toffee Town,*
> *To fight the famous Wolves,*
> *A team of English renown.*
> *The Toffees came on boldly,*
> *Their victory for to seek;*
> *But now they go home gravely*
> *O'er their troubles for to weep.*
> *Farewell, farewell, dear old Everton,*
> *No more for the Pot you will dribble;*
> *You have lost it today through difficult play*
> *And we'll shout farewell for ever and ever.*

— PEP-TALK TURNAROUND —

'I was the whipping boy at Wembley, where Eddie Gray gave me the biggest run-around of my life. He gave me a mummy and a daddy of a chasing, and my confidence was at an all-time low at the end of the match. I was half-expecting Dave Sexton to drop me for the replay, but he motivated me with a terrific pep-talk and I was determined not to put a foot wrong at Old Trafford. To score the winning goal was the stuff dreams are made of. I've never seen a team as devastated as Leeds at the end. They'd had a magnificent season and finished with nothing to show for it.'
– Chelsea's David Webb reflects on his side's eventual win in the 1970 Cup final.

— APPEARANCES IN THE FINAL —

Competition proper 1871–72 to 2004–05:

— THE GUNNERS WARM UP —

If Arsenal were hoping for a gentle run-out in their last League game before appearing in the 1930 Cup final, Herbert Chapman's men were sorely disappointed. Their match against Leicester City at Highbury ended in a breathless 6–6 draw. Despite this, the Gunners had just enough left in the tank to put two past Huddersfield at Wembley to secure their first major honour.

— THE UNBEATABLE ENGINEERS —

Although they lost the first two Cup finals they appeared in, Royal Engineers could be forgiven for thinking those defeats were little more than an unfortunate blip. Indeed, they were two of just three matches they lost out of the 86 they played between 1872 and 1875. During this time they scored an astonishing 244 goals, conceding only 21. They eventually won the Cup in 1875, beating Old Etonians 2–0.

— FOOTBALL CRAZY —

Such was the growing popularity of football among the working classes, in 1913 it was suggested that the British economy was suffering, with too many workmen spending too much time watching football matches.

Critics pointed to the fact that a British shipping firm had decided to have three large steamers built in France due to the refusal of shipbuilding hands in this country to work full time. Research demonstrated that 18.8 per cent of possible working time was being lost, chiefly through workers going to football matches. There were, indeed, some whopping attendances: that year the Cup final at Crystal Palace was witnessed by more than 120,000 spectators.

— GALLANT SOUTHPORT STOPPED SHORT —

Every Cup competition throws up one or more no-hopers who punch above their weight and give the big teams a bloody nose in the process. In 1931 it was Southport's turn. The side from the depths of Division Three (North) took the scalps of Millwall, Blackpool and Bradford en route to a quarter-final encounter with Everton at Goodison Park. But while Everton may have been in the Second Division, they still had, in Dixie Dean, one of the game's great goal-scorers. Having notched four against Crystal Palace in the previous round, Dean did not disappoint this time, banging home another four as the Toffees ran out convincing 9–1 winners.

— PLAYING FOR THEIR LIVES —

Being on the brink of financial meltdown is not a new phenomenon for football clubs, but rarely has the line between life and death been so acute as it was in 1931 for Halifax Town. After nearly ten years of scraping by on FA handouts and fund-raising appeals, the Yorkshiremen knew that the only way they could possibly survive another season was with a decent FA Cup run.

So it was that their first-round tie away to Newark Town in November had an extra frisson of drama: if they lost, Halifax would not only go out of the Cup, they would in all probability go out of existence.

A game riven with tension did not start well for the visitors, as Newark took the lead after just a few minutes. Halifax equalised, and so began a second half which is best summed up by what was subsequently written in the Shaymen's official history:

'One of the tensest struggles I have ever seen followed. Town had to defend as if for dear life – they simply dare not lose – while Newark attacked like furies. In the last 15 minutes the suspense was almost unbearable, and when someone handed a cigarette to Benny Wheelhouse, who, unfit, was watching the game from the touchline, he chewed it up and ate it in his excitement.'

Halifax hung on to draw, and in the replay beat Newark 2–1. In the second round they overcame Accrington, which meant that while they were beaten in round three by Bournemouth, they had secured the vital funds to survive.

— BRIGHTON'S BALLS-UP —

Despite being a League club, Brighton were forced to play in the qualifying rounds of the 1932 competition because someone at the club forgot to claim their right to join at the first-round stage. In the end they played 11 games and reached the fifth round – five more than when they progressed to the FA Cup final in 1983.

— CLASH OF THE TITANS —

It was billed as the Championship of the World, but nobody south of the border seriously expected an upset when English Cup winners West Bromwich Albion took on Scottish holders Renton in 1888. West Brom had toppled a strong Preston side 2–1, which was seen as a somewhat heftier achievement than Renton's 6–1 hammering of Cambuslang. But knockout football is nothing if not perverse, and there were red faces all round as the Scots ran out 2–0 winners to become the first official World Club Champions.

— BREACH OF ETIQUETTE —

One of football's unwritten rules is that when a player is injured, his team should kick the ball into touch and will then be given it back from the resulting throw-in.

But the rule is, after all, unwritten.

During their sixth-round tie against Arsenal in 1999, Sheffield United were the side with a man down and the ball was duly booted into Row Z. Arsenal took the throw, but instead of passing it back, they started a move which led to Marc Overmars scoring the decisive goal.

United complained, but the referee had no option but to shrug his shoulders. After all, technically no offence had been committed. The Gunners won 2–1, but in the resulting backlash the FA ordered a replay at Highbury. Arsenal again won 2–1, with Overmars once more on the scoresheet.

— RENTON SHOCK —

The last year Scottish clubs took part in the FA Cup was 1887, and they duly signed off with a shock upset when little Renton beat the mighty Blackburn Rovers 2–0 in the second round. Everybody was so stunned, they almost failed to notice that newcomers Glasgow Rangers reached the semi-finals.

— A CREEPY COINCIDENCE? —

In 1955–56, Leeds United were drawn at home to Cardiff City in the third round and, after a goalless first half, Cardiff ran out winners by 2–1.

The following year, Leeds were again drawn at home to Cardiff in the third round and, after another goalless first half, the Welshmen again finished 2–1 winners.

As you might imagine, there was some rather perplexed scratching of heads when the draw for the third round was made in 1957–58 and Leeds were once more drawn at home to Cardiff.

A crowd of more than 30,000 people packed into Elland Road to see if the improbable could occur. Few believed it would, because whereas Cardiff and Leeds were in the First and Second Divisions respectively back in 1955, two years later the roles were reversed and Leeds were very much in the ascendancy.

But once again the Cup proved to be no respecter of League status. In icy conditions, the Welshmen took the lead, Alan Harrington blasting home from long range after 20 minutes. Bobby Forrest equalised for Leeds, but to everyone's amazement the underdogs scrambled home a second just before half-time.

And 2–1 is how it stayed – although Leeds had a legitimate penalty appeal turned down in the dying minutes of the match.

It was the sixth time in ten successive seasons that United had been dumped out of the Cup in the third round, and the third defeat by Cardiff City. Although Leeds would beat Cardiff on the other four occasions they would be drawn together in the Cup, a shiver of fear still travels the length of the M1 (and beyond) whenever the Bluebirds are drawn out of the bag.

— LIGHTS, ACTION . . . —

The first FA Cup match to be played under floodlights was a preliminary round replay between Kidderminster Harriers and Brierley Hill Alliance in 1955. Not to be outdone, in the same year Carlisle United also played Darlington under lights at Brunton Park. Until then the FA had outlawed floodlights, primarily because they wanted games to be played on Saturday afternoons, but also because the artificial illumination had never worked satisfactorily.

— TRICKERY BETWEEN THE STICKS —

Sixty-two years before Bruce Grobbelaar's infamous 'wobbly legs' antics against Roma in the 1984 European Cup final, another goalkeeper was in the headlines for using off-putting tactics to distract a penalty-taker.

His name was James Mitchell, and he was between the sticks for Preston North End in the 1922 FA Cup final when Huddersfield Town were awarded a spot-kick. As penalty-taker Billy Smith prepared himself, Mitchell – an amateur who wore spectacles and a bandeau (headband) – started jumping up and down and waving his arms in the air, according to one contemporary account, 'like an excited monkey on a stick awaiting the offer of a bag of peanuts'.

It made no difference to Smith, who duly hammered the ball home to give Huddersfield a 1–0 win. The following season the FA issued an edict which banned goalkeepers from moving until the ball was kicked.

— CANTONA MISSES OUT – BUT NOT FOR LONG —

Football can be a capricious game. In 1994 Eric Cantona was the toast of Wembley after bagging two goals in Manchester United's 4–0 drubbing of Chelsea. When United returned for the final against Everton a year later, the enigmatic Frenchman was missing – he'd been banned for eight months for karate-kicking a Crystal Palace fan earlier that season. In 1996 he was back, scoring the winner as United beat Liverpool 1–0, securing their second League and FA Cup double in three years.

— SAM'S PREDICTION —

'It'll never go back to London!'
- Sam Warburton, captain of Cup-winners Blackburn Olympic
  in 1883. For 15 years his prophecy appeared to have come
  true as teams from the North and Midlands monopolised the
  trophy until 1896.

— ARSENAL AWAY —

Arsenal were drawn away from home in every round of
their 1971 League and FA Cup double-winning season
and, astonishingly, the same thing happened when they
battled their way to the final the following year. This
time they were pipped at Wembley by Leeds United.

— THE FASTEST GOAL —

Roberto Di Matteo's 43-second thunderbolt against
Middlesbrough is correctly credited as the fastest FA Cup final
goal at Wembley. But the quickest Cup final goal ever was
scored by Aston Villa's Bob Chatt, who netted after 30 seconds
in the 1895 final.

— PLAYER-MANAGERS —

Four men have appeared in FA Cup finals as player-managers.
They are Kenny Dalglish for Liverpool (1986 v Everton), Glenn
Hoddle for Chelsea (1994 v Manchester United), Gianluca Vialli
for Chelsea (1997 v Middlesbrough) and Dennis Wise for
Millwall (2004 v Manchester United).

— A FISHY TALE OF SUCCESS —

When Great Yarmouth Town reached the first round in
1954, their reward was a plum home tie against Crystal
Palace. The only problem was, Yarmouth's ground was far
too small to accommodate everyone who wanted to see
the game. Not to be deterred, club officials got together
with the local fishing community, and built a series of
terraces out of fish boxes. Their industry was rewarded as
a single goal by Rackham secured a famous victory.

— THE BRITISH WAY —

'Suddenly there is a hush. Every cap and hat is removed as the band begins playing the most moving of all hymns, *Abide With Me*. Then women and children from the grimy streets of the industrial town are at last on common ground with those from the stately homes of England. What does it matter if they are off-key or are not quite sure of the words? Who takes notice if a few tears are shed? Who need be ashamed of keeping silent because emotion will not allow otherwise? I think it is a wonderful thing, and one for which British sports lovers, regardless of politics and creed, are to be respected.'
– Bert Trautmann, German-born goalkeeper, *Steppes To Wembley* (1956).

— PORTERFIELD – ONE–NIL! —

Cup shocks abounded in the 1970s, but few were greeted with such nationwide satisfaction as Sunderland's 1973 Wembley win over Leeds. It wasn't so much that Sunderland were a Second Division side flirting with relegation as the fact that Don Revie's Yorkshiremen were almost universally reviled for their hard-man tactics and alleged rule-bending.

The sole goal was scored by Ian Porterfield – although the match is remembered more for Jim Montgomery's amazing double save and the sight of manager Bob Stokoe running across the pitch in his trilby and raincoat to embrace the goalkeeping hero at the end of the match.

— PLAY TO THE WHISTLE —

The first all-Midlands final in 1887 was a tense affair which remained goalless until the second half, when Aston Villa winger Arthur Hodgetts raced on to a through pass and banged the ball between the sticks to open the scoring. West Bromwich Albion goalkeeper Roberts was not unduly bothered. Assuming Hodgetts was offside, he stepped aside and allowed the Villa man to score unimpeded. To his horror, the umpires on both sides of the pitch ruled that Hodgetts was onside and that the goal should stand. Albion never recovered from this blunder and lost 2–0.

— THE ORIGINAL CUP —

The first FA Challenge Cup was designed and made in silver by Martin, Hall & Co at a cost of £20. Known as 'the little tin idol', it was 18ins high, had a capacity of one quart, and lasted for 24 years before it was stolen.

— AN ENGLISH IRISHMAN —

League and Cup double winners Liverpool recorded their Wembley triumph in 1986 with only one player who was born in England – and he was Republic of Ireland defender Mark Lawrenson, who first saw the light of day in Preston.

— KEEGAN'S CHANGE OF HEART —

'I had sunk into a mood of feeling there was surely more to life than football, but my appetite for the game was restored by a match in which nearly everything worked to perfection for me. There had been times when I had played better, but what made the difference was that I had Wembley as my stage and millions of television viewers as my audience.'

– Kevin Keegan, who scored two of Liverpool's three goals against Newcastle United in the one-sided 1974 Cup final.

— SUPER SANDY —

During Tottenham Hotspur's triumphant 1900–01 FA Cup campaign the undisputed star of the show was Scottish goal-machine Sandy Brown. His phenomenal record began when he scored four in the replayed first-round tie against Preston North End.

In the second round he bagged both as Spurs beat Bury 2–1, followed by two against Reading in the third, four in the semi-final against West Brom and three in the replayed final against Sheffield United.

In all he scored 15 of Spurs' 20 goals, becoming the first player to register in every round, and his total is still the highest in a single FA Cup run.

— ALL-ROUND GREAT —

Playing right-back for Southampton in the 1902 final against Sheffield United was the great C B Fry. But then, what major sporting occasion took place without him in those days? Fry was truly a sporting phenomenon, an England cricketer, international footballer, long-jump record holder, rugby player – the list of his achievements is worthy of a book in itself.

Had he scored the winning goal and lifted the FA Cup that day, few would have been surprised. But on this occasion, Fry missed out. After the first match was drawn, Southampton lost the replay 2–1, their second successive final defeat.

— AN EARLY SHOCK —

Newcastle United's travails against non-League Cup opposition reached a peak of humiliation against Hereford in 1972, but the Magpies' shakiness against footballing tiddlers was in evidence much earlier. In 1907 Newcastle won the League for the second time in three years but their hopes of a double were scuppered in the first round by lowly Crystal Palace, who were then languishing near the bottom of the Southern League. In front of a stunned crowd of 40,000 at St James's Park, the Londoners scored early and hung on for a remarkable win.

— LIVERPOOL TURFED OUT OF THE CUP —

There are many who believe that the advent of the Premiership and its squads of highly paid 'galacticos' has all but ended the chances of Cup giant-killers achieving their moment of glory.

But the old competition still has a way of making a monkey out of the mightiest of top-flight giants, as Liverpool found to their cost in the third round in 2004–05.

Liverpool were drawn away to Second Division strugglers Burnley. It was manager Rafael Benitez's first season in charge at Anfield, and while the Spaniard's decision to omit a host of first-team regulars – including Steven Gerrard and Jamie Carragher – made sense, it showed that he clearly hadn't realised how the Cup can make a mockery of the form book.

On a boggy Turf Moor pitch on a cold January night, Liverpool's weakened team was given the run-around by a Burnley side bursting with enthusiasm. The only goal was thoroughly deserved in every sense; instead of making a routine goal-line clearance, Liverpool's Djimi Traore attempted a risky back-flick and ended up prodding the ball into his own net.

Liverpool were unable to claw back an equaliser and were bundled humiliatingly out of the Cup at the first hurdle.

— HOW IT WORKS —

The FA Cup is played over eight months, but the mechanics of ensuring the competition runs smoothly is a year-long process, beginning when the relevant dates for the fixtures are established.

This is a complex business, because midweek replays must not clash with European tournaments, internationals and League Cup ties. Entry forms for the following year are sent out from January onwards, going automatically to those who have already competed, while first-time entrants must apply.

Completed entry forms and entry fee must be returned by 1 April.

No clubs – not even the Premiership aristocrats – are allowed to enter without first submitting a form. Entries are scrutinised by the Challenge Cup committee, with facilities, gates, results, etc., being considered to ensure that standards are not lowered.

The draw for the first four rounds takes place in early July.

— GRUBBY OLD CUP —

Arsenal's last-ditch win over Manchester United in the 1979 final will go down as one of the most dramatic Wembley climaxes of all time. However, not everyone was overawed by the silverware. When Gunners manager Terry Neill took the trophy home with him, his daughters described it as 'a grubby old cup' – and a few minutes later the stunned Neill found them washing it in a neighbour's swimming pool!

— SHARED ACCOMMODATION —

Aston Villa and Everton each booked into a 'secret' London hotel in preparation for the 1897 final – only to bump into each other in reception. After sharing a convivial evening, the two sides took to the pitch the following afternoon and Villa won 3–2.

— CHESTERFIELD DENIED —

Whenever the thorny question of goal-line cameras is raised, you can bet that everyone in Chesterfield is in favour. Having magnificently reached the semi-finals in 1997, the side from the Second Division sensationally went two goals up against Premiership outfit Middlesbrough.

Already on their knees, 'Boro would have been out for the count if Chesterfield's third strike had been allowed, with the score at 2–1. Instead, the referee David Elleray ruled that the shot had hit the bar and rebounded outside the goal-line.

TV replays suggested the effort was valid – but 'Boro were handed their lifeline and duly clawed their way back to lead 3–2 in extra time.

The drama was not over yet, though, and with just a minute left Chesterfield equalised.

The replay, sadly, did not live up to the first match, the minnows being beaten 3–0 and left to dream about what might have been had technology been on their side at the crucial time. Middlesbrough, meanwhile, were beaten 2–0 by Chelsea in a one-sided final.

— MACCA'S FINAL APPEARANCE —

Although they were from Merseyside, the Beatles never professed a great interest in football and when asked if they supported Liverpool or Everton always studiously avoided the question. However, in 1968, Paul McCartney made a surprise appearance in the FA Cup final crowd to see Everton lose 1–0 to West Bromwich Albion. He also became the first Beatle to play at Wembley – although it was during Live Aid in 1985.

— MONEY FOR NOTHING —

'We interviewed the treasurer as occasion arose . . .'
– Fergie Suter of Blackburn Rovers in 1884, explaining how he and his team got around the fact that professionalism would not be legalised until 1885.

— MUTUAL APPRECIATION —

'We have won the Cup, but the glory is yours.'
– Newcastle United director-manager Stan Seymour to ten-man Arsenal after their brave display in losing 1–0 in the 1952 final.

'Joe Mercer is the greatest player I have ever met in the game.'
– United captain Joe Harvey on his opposing skipper, who inspired his depleted side for 90 minutes.

'Boys, I have never been so proud of you in victory as I am in defeat.'
– Arsenal boss Tom Whittaker after the 1952 Wembley loss.

— A PHOENIX TAKES WING —

On 6 February 1958, the cream of Manchester United's young players, eight of the so-called Busby Babes, were wiped out in the Munich air crash. Yet just 13 days later, a United team took to the pitch again, this time in the fifth round of the FA Cup.

The opponents were Sheffield Wednesday, and one can only imagine how they felt as a crowd of 60,000 – many in tears – welcomed a scratch team of reserves, juniors, hastily imported reinforcements and, in goalkeeper Harry Gregg and right-back Bill Foulkes, two survivors of the crash.

'A Phoenix takes wing' is how one journalist described the match, which United won 3–0. But it did not end there. Carried along by a wave of emotion and national goodwill, United somehow beat West Bromwich Albion and Fulham to make it to Wembley.

Having been beaten in the Matthews final five years earlier, Bolton Wanderers were in no mood to roll over again, however, and two goals from Nat Lofthouse secured their win in front of 100,000 people.

But if Bolton had at last won the trophy, there was no doubt which team had won the hearts of the nation. The Phoenix had indeed taken wing.

— THE FIRST GREATS —

In 1881, *Boy's Own Paper* printed a list of what it considered to be the 18 leading players in the first decade of the FA Cup. They were:

• **Charles Campbell** (captain of Queen's Park and Scotland, FA Cup finalist 1884 and 1885)

• **Charles Caborn** (played in Nottingham Forest's first Cup tie, against Notts County in 1878)

• **Tom Marshall** (Darwen, Blackburn Olympic and England)

• **Harry Swepstone** (Pilgrims and England, founder member of the Corinthians)

• **Jack Hunter** (Wednesday, FA Cup winner with Blackburn Olympic 1883, Blackburn Rovers and England)

• **Sam Weller Widdowson** (Nottingham Forest and England, inventor of shinguards)

• **Edwin Luntley** (Nottingham Forest, member of their first Cup side, and England)

• **James Frederick McLeod Prinsep** (youngest FA Cup finalist, aged 17 years 245 days, for Clapham Rovers in 1879; Cup winner with Old Carthusians in 1881, and England)

• **Harry McNeil** (Queen's Park and Scotland)

• **William Lindsay** (Cup winner with Wanderers 1876, 1877, 1878, and England)

• **John Sands** (England goalkeeper and another of Forest's Cup team)

• **Tom Brindle** (Darwen, Blackburn Olympic and England)

• **William Mosforth** (Sheffield Wednesday, Sheffield United and England)

• **Francis Sparks** (Cup winner with Clapham Rovers 1880, and England)

- **Herbert Whitfield** (Cup winner with Old Etonians 1879, finalist 1881, and England)

- **Norman Bailey** (Old Westminsters, Cup finalist with Clapham Rovers 1879, Cup winner 1880, Corinthians, Wanderers and England)

- **Edward Bambridge** (Upton Park, Clapham Rovers, Swifts and England, later secretary of Corinthians)

- **F W Earp** (played in Forest's first Cup tie in 1878)

— SILVER NOT COPPER —

After a tie in 1882, Long Eaton Rangers from Derbyshire handed Sheffield Wednesday their £4 share of the gate money in two bags containing nearly a thousand old pennies. Wednesday refused the shrapnel and, after a prolonged argument, were eventually paid in silver.

— DUAL INTERNATIONALS —

Only 12 men have played both football and cricket at full international level for England, and two of them turned out for Everton in the 1906 Cup final against Newcastle. Their names were Jack Sharp and Harry Makepeace, and between them they amassed nearly 80 centuries for Lancashire. Right-winger Sharp, in particular, was the torment of United that day, providing the cross from which Sandy Young scored the winner in the 75th minute.

Makepeace was a right-half who, while never flashy, was regarded as a model of consistency in both sports. Indeed, he is the only man to have pocketed a Cup-winner's medal, a League Championship medal and a County Championship medal.

— BETTER THINGS TO DO —

In 1880 Aston Villa pulled out of their FA Cup second-round tie against Oxford University because it clashed with what they regarded as a far more prestigious match in the Birmingham Senior Cup.

— CHANGING TIMES —

'One may justifiably wonder how Charles Alcock, Sir Francis Marindin and those who sat together on July 20 1871 in that small room in *The Sportsman* office, would view the results of their handiwork [in 1930]. They would probably have been rather frightened by it all. The five-figure transfer fee had already arrived when, in October 1928, Arsenal paid Bolton Wanderers £10,890 for David Jack; the approach of the Cup competition had brought special training and special diet for the players, now, like racehorses for the Derby, timed to reach a peak of fitness at a given moment; champagne had been given to the players of Preston North End at half-time in a semi-final tie against the Spurs; ahead lay gland treatment. All this and more would sorely perplex Alcock and his fellows. Nor would they grasp immediately the significance of a national competition which had once been little more than a parochial tournament.'
– Geoffrey Green, *The Official History of the FA Cup*.

— STAR BILLING —

In the days before cruises, win bonuses and all-expenses-paid holidays, Wednesday's 1907 Cup-winning side were rewarded with a stage appearance at Sheffield's music hall alongside top entertainer George Robey.

— THE TOP AND BOTTOM OF IT —

As far as FA Cup shocks go, Wrexham's 2–1 win over mighty Arsenal in a third-round tie in 1992 must rate among the most sensational.

Arsenal led through an Alan Smith goal until seven minutes from time, when veteran Mickey Thomas fired an unstoppable free-kick past David Seaman. Cue traditional FA Cup third-round mayhem, culminating in a scrambled winner by Wrexham's Steve Watkins.

The result was also a cause for celebration among Cup statisticians: it was the first time the club finishing bottom of the Football League in the previous season had knocked out the League champions.

— CURSE OF THE CUP FINAL 'KEEPER —

Just a year after Manchester City's Bert Trautmann had been carried from the Wembley pitch nursing a broken neck, disaster struck another Manchester goalkeeper in the FA Cup final.

His name was Ray Wood, and he was in goal for Manchester United in the 1957 final against Aston Villa. Only six minutes into the game, Wood collided with Villa's left-winger Peter McParland in one of the regular barging incidents that the rules still allowed in those days.

Wood hit the deck and it was quickly established that he had broken his cheekbone. Of course, substitutes were not allowed, so centre-half Jackie Blanchflower was handed the goalkeeper's jersey. Despite making a string of gallant saves, Blanchflower was beaten twice – both times, ironically, by McParland – as Villa ran out 2–1 winners. Wood, incidentally, reappeared on the wing for the last seven minutes of the match.

— FROM BALL BOYS TO THE KING —

Sir Stanley Rous was an admirable successor to Charles Alcock as England's 'Mr Football'. FA secretary from 1934 to 1961 and then president of FIFA for 13 years, Rous was also Cup final referee in 1934. His experience that day was to prove revelatory.

'Arrangements were haphazard,' he recalled in 1978. 'No-one had met my linesmen or me or told us where to find the dressing rooms. We found we had to change in an office, and at the game's end there was no bath for us so we begged one off the winning team.'

Immediately upon becoming FA secretary, Rous decided that things needed a shake-up and he duly sat down and wrote a comprehensive guide to procedure behind the scenes on Cup final day, covering all the timings and responsibilities regarding guests and officials. At Lancaster Gate, home of the FA, the book became known as *From Ball Boys To The King* and became the standard reference work for the next 50 years.

— 15 APRIL 1989 —

It was supposed to be one of the great days in the footballing calendar. Instead, the 1989 FA Cup semi-final between Liverpool and Nottingham Forest became infamous as the worst disaster in the history of British sport.

Hillsborough, home of Sheffield Wednesday, was a traditional semi-final venue, and the Leppings Lane end had been occupied for the day by Liverpool fans in buoyant mood. Yet as kick-off approached, it was clear that things were going terribly wrong.

Fans attempting to get into the ground at the last minute caused those at the front of the terracing to be crushed against fencing which had been installed, with dreadful irony, to prevent fans spilling on to the pitch, to combat pitch invasions and hooliganism.

The tragedy unfolded in front of a live TV audience of millions, and few who saw the sight of bodies being dragged away on makeshift stretchers fashioned from advertising hoardings will ever forget it.

Ninety-five people died that day, and football entered one of its gravest periods of introspection. There were calls for the Cup to be abandoned, even for the trophy to be retired for good.

In the end, Merseyside would unite at Wembley that year as Liverpool and Everton contested an emotional final. Fittingly, it was Liverpool who won a stirring game 3–2, with Ian Rush scoring twice.

— SEMI-FINAL GOAL BLITZ —

FA Cup semi-finals are notoriously edgy affairs with few chances and even fewer goals. This was not the case in 1990, however, when the two ties produced an astonishing 13 goals between them. In both cases, lower division opposition pulled out all the stops against bigger clubs. Oldham Athletic drew 3–3 with Manchester United, while Crystal Palace produced one of the upsets of all time by beating mighty Liverpool 4–3, netting the winner in the 109th minute of an epic encounter at Villa Park.

— DREAMLAND FOR TAYLOR —

'I can't help thinking that I am dreaming all this. It seems like only yesterday that I was playing with Rochdale in front of 3,000 supporters.'
– West Ham's Alan Taylor after scoring both goals in the 1975 Cup final against Fulham.

— THE OLD 1–2–7 FORMATION —

The idea of football being a game of defence and attack was unheard of in the 1870s. When Wanderers played Royal Engineers in the first Cup final, both teams lined up with a goalkeeper, one full-back and two half-backs in defence, while up front there were no fewer than seven attackers spread out across the pitch.

It should have produced a goal feast – but as early results show, all too often games ended up being midfield free-for-alls with goal chances being few and far between. Dribblers were highly sought-after, but then so were cloggers with the ability to kick them off the ball.

— UNITED'S CUP OF CHEER —

The FA Cup has often provided a turning point in the fortunes of Manchester United. Their win in 1990 arguably saved manager Alex Ferguson from the sack and sparked their subsequent domination of the domestic game throughout the next decade, in which they won the Premiership five times and the European Champions League in 1999.

It was a similar story in 1963. Despite a team which contained the likes of Denis Law, Pat Crerand and Bobby Charlton, United were languishing near the relegation zone when they arrived at Wembley to play high-flying Leicester City.

United upset the form book, winning 3–1 with goals from Law and a brace from David Herd – and from that day they never looked back, going on to win the League Championship in 1965 and 1967, as well as the European Cup against Benfica in 1968.

— BIRD'S-EYE SOLUTION —

In 1936 Wembley bosses were in dispute with the newsreel companies over broadcasting rights and as a result barred them from the stadium for the Cup final between Arsenal and Sheffield United. With the sort of ingenuity modern-day paparazzi would be proud of, the companies chartered a fleet of auto-giro helicopters to get a bird's-eye view of the match – scrupulously keeping out of Wembley airspace, of course.

— DARWEN DIG DEEP —

For the first seven years of its existence the FA Cup was very much a closed shop, reserved for teams in London and the South-East of England. Queen's Park were from Glasgow, but their progress to the later rounds was often hampered by work commitments and the sheer cost of having to travel to London to honour their fixtures.

In 1879, however, a team of mill workers from the Lancashire town of Darwen showed what the Cup was all about when they drew the mighty Old Etonians at Kennington Oval.

A local whip-round raised the necessary funds to send the team to London where, despite being 5–1 down with 20 minutes left, the underdogs staged one of the all-time great recoveries to tie the match 5–5.

That meant a replay, and as replays took place at the same ground it meant that the folk of Darwen once again had to dig deep for the £175 required to send their boys to London, though this time they were augmented by a donation of £15 from the FA and the Etonians.

Incredibly, the second game ended 2–2. A week later Darwen were back in the capital, where they were beaten 6–2. The disappointment at the defeat back home was no doubt tempered by the fact that the Lancastrians no longer had to fork out their own money to keep their boys in the Cup.

— THE TRIUMPH OF THE OLD STYLE —

'Bolton Wanderers, by winning the FA Cup a third time in seven years, earned a new nickname. They are now likely to be known as the "3–6–9's" instead of the Trotters. They won the Cup in 1923, 1926 and 1929 and gave an improved display in each match. One thing was proved beyond question in 1929 and that was that the old style of football, with the forwards all in a line, can still be exploited successfully, for after Bolton had failed to score with the exaggerated "W" formation they resorted to the old style and won. What was still more pleasing to Englishmen was that their team included no fewer than eight English-born players.'
– *Daily Express*, 1929.

— A CORKING CUP RECORD —

Alan Cork's goal for Sheffield United in the Cup semi-final derby against Sheffield Wednesday in 1993 must have brought back distant memories. It was nearly 15 years since he had scored his first FA Cup goal – for Wimbledon against Gravesend in November 1978. Cork, who was a Cup winner with the Dons in 1988, would end on the losing side this time. Wednesday won 2–1 and went through to the final where they were eventually beaten by Arsenal in a replay.

— STORMIN' NORMAN —

Wembley was a happy hunting ground for Manchester United's Norman Whiteside. At the age of 18 years and 19 days he became the youngest player to score in an FA Cup final when his replay header in 1983 helped to scupper Brighton's brave effort as the Reds ran out 4–0 winners.

Two years later Whiteside struck again, this time in extra time against Everton. Little seemed to be on when the Irishman collected the ball on the right corner of the penalty area. But, with a quick look up, Whiteside curled the ball with his left foot beyond the outstretched hand of Neville Southall and into the far corner of the net.

The Cup belonged to United – despite the fact that they had been reduced to ten men by the sending-off of Kevin Moran.

— RICKY VILLA'S DRIBBLE —

In 1981 Argentinian import Ricky Villa had played so poorly in the drawn 100th FA Cup final against Manchester City that he was substituted. There would be no repeat of this in the replay as Villa scored twice in an historic Tottenham win. Villa's second has rightly gone down in Cup folklore as one of the best goals ever seen.

1. Ricky Villa wins possession.

2. He evades Tommy Caton's challenge as he swerves into the box.

3. Another swerve takes him past Ray Ranson's tackle.

4. Having made space now, Villa attempts to find a shooting chance.

5. City 'keeper Joe Corrigan advances to narrow the angle . . .

6. . . . but Villa somehow lifts the ball over his body and into the corner of the net.

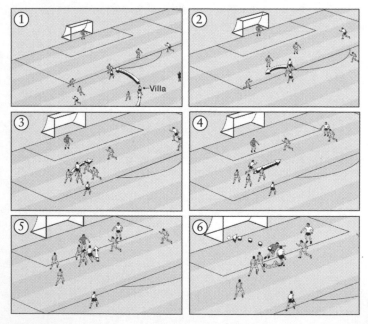

— PENALTY SHOOT-OUT —

In 1991 the police decided that there should be a minimum of ten days between a Cup tie and its replay. This effectively meant an end to unlimited replays and the introduction of penalty shoot-outs if the first and only replay was not settled in extra time. In its first season the shoot-out lottery claimed the scalps of both Manchester United and Newcastle United, while Portsmouth were heartbreakingly eliminated after holding Liverpool in two tight games. Pompey boss Jim Smith spoke for many when he described shoot-outs as trivialising the competition.

— TRIUMPH AND DISASTER FOR THE DOC —

Having lost in the final as a player with Preston North End (1954) and as a manager with both Chelsea (1967) and Manchester United (1976), Tommy Docherty – who had also tasted Wembley defeat four times in Scotland's colours – had reason to believe the FA Cup had not treated him kindly. So even the most hard-hearted football fan might secretly have shared the outspoken Glaswegian's moment of triumph when he finally led Manchester United to a famous win over Liverpool in 1977.

The Doc being the Doc, however, his moment of glory was only short-lived. Just two months after the Wembley final, he was on his way out of Old Trafford in disgrace after revealing that he was having an affair with Mary Brown, wife of the United physiotherapist.

'I am the first manager to be sacked for falling in love,' he complained.

— WORLD SERVICE —

Among the listeners to the first Cup final radio commentary in 1927 were residents in Kenya Colony, Mount Lawley in Australia and the Naga Hills in Assam. The *Radio Times* commented: 'It is not too much to say that the Cup final commentary plays its part in welding the Empire together.'

— REFEREE STRIKES AGAIN —

The normally mild-mannered Graham Taylor was not one to speak ill of anyone, let alone the referee. But in 1987 the then Watford manager let his opinion be known in no uncertain terms when Brian Stevens was appointed to officiate in the Hornets' quarter-final tie with Arsenal. Earlier in the season Stevens had controversially sent off Watford 'keeper Tony Coton in a League match against the Gunners, and Taylor went public with his view that the same ref should not be in charge of the Cup tie.

In the end, Stevens refereed – and Taylor would be grateful that he did.

Late in the game Watford were leading 2–1 when Steve Sims challenged Arsenal's rangy striker Niall Quinn in the penalty area. Quinn went down like a felled tree and, as one, the Arsenal players raised their hands to appeal for a penalty. Linesman Graham Crafter also raised his flag, but, possibly because it got lost in the sea of yellow shirts behind him, referee Stevens didn't see the signal. Instead, he waved away the appeals and allowed play to continue. Watford duly went up the other end of the field, where Luther Blissett scored his second goal of the day to make it 3–1.

Surrounded by furious Arsenal players, Stevens consulted with his linesman – but after a lengthy debate the goal was allowed to stand and Watford were through to the semi-final, on their way to a Wembley showdown with Everton.

Taylor, wisely, kept his counsel about the referee.

— RETURN OF THE WANDERER —

Spurs celebrated their 1921 Cup final win over Wolves by tying the same blue-and-white ribbons to the trophy that they had used after winning the competition 20 years earlier. One bemused London reporter wrote: 'The Cup returns to the south, like a wanderer from strange lands, beaming on London with its silver arms akimbo and still wondering why it is that only one southern professional club has ever given it hospitality.'

— INJURY CRISIS —

When Leicester City right-back Len Chalmers was carried off in the 18th minute of the 1961 final against Tottenham Hotspur, it was the seventh time in nine years that English football's gala day at Wembley had been marred by injury. Despite this, it would be another six years before substitutes would be permitted.

— OUT IN FORCE —

Times have changed since the Cup final was covered by a couple of Movietone cameras. For the 2005 final between Arsenal and Manchester United, the BBC alone used:

- Thirty-eight cameras, including three 'super slo-mo' devices for enhanced replay action; two 'steadycams' carried on frames on the backs of camera operators running up and down pitchside for all the touchline action; and 12 'large lenses' for close-ups of players' faces and the ref's decisions.

- More than 14 miles of cable linking cameras and mikes in the Millennium Stadium to the BBC production vehicles outside.

- More than 30 special-effects mikes capturing all the sound in the stadium.

- Two helicopters carrying cameras looking down over the stadium and Cardiff city.

- The BBC Sport blimp floating 1,000 feet in the sky for aerial views of the surrounding area.

- Two cameras on the backs of motorbikes following the team coaches as they arrived.

— PRESTON GOAL MACHINE —

In the 1887–88 season, Preston North End scored 51 goals in six FA Cup ties, including a record 26 against hapless Hyde. Unfortunately they could only manage one in the final, as West Bromwich Albion ran out 2–1 winners.

— THE DOUBLE – OF SORTS —

By beating Midlands rivals Birmingham City 2–1 in the 1931 FA Cup final, West Bromwich Albion became the first club to win the Cup and secure promotion from the Second Division in the same season. Their chairman was Billy Bassett, an Albion Cup-winner in 1888 and 1892 at the Oval.

— A SHINING EXAMPLE —

'A treasured recollection is one of those fine exhibitions of sportsmanship that really mark the great man. It occurred in the replayed Cup Final on the Manchester United ground at Old Trafford between Bradford City and Newcastle United in 1911. Colin Veitch, the Newcastle captain, had collided heavily with Thompson, the little Irishman of Bradford City, who was knocked out. Veitch himself was not much the worse, and his side was in grave danger and needed his help, but he made the great sacrifice of assisting his smaller opponent while Bradford City were actually scoring the winning goal, and when the end came he slipped quietly across to Spiers, the City captain, to be the first to congratulate him. I wrote at the time: "Those of us who observed saw the sportsman rising superior to the mere man, the spirit of camaraderie shining brightly at a time when another might have been wrangling with the referee."'

– V A S Beanland, *Great Games and Great Players* (1945).

— OOPS! —

'I shall never forget the night I dropped the FA Cup – and smashed it. Charlton won this most envied of all soccer trophies in 1947 and I planned to take it myself to the welcome-home reception. But while opening the door of my car and, at the same time, balancing the Cup, I dropped the lid and found to my horror that the top had broken off. There was little time to spare, so I called at a garage and explained my predicament. The mechanics were soon working with their soldering irons and, at the reception, not a soul apart from myself knew about the accident. Next day I arranged for a silversmith to do a really first class job on it.'

– Jimmy Seed, Charlton manager.

— THE HAMILTON INCIDENT —

In 1977 Liverpool, under quietly spoken but inspirational manager Bob Paisley, were going for an unprecedented treble of League, FA Cup and European Cup. In the event they would have to make do with the title and European glory after going down 2–1 to Manchester United in the FA Cup final.

Perhaps they used up all their luck in a tumultuous semi-final against Merseyside rivals Everton at Maine Road.

In a typically partisan encounter, Liverpool took the lead through an exquisite Terry McDermott chip – an effort which would later be voted *Match of the Day*'s goal of the season. But Everton levelled through Duncan McKenzie and after Jimmy Case restored Liverpool's lead, Bruce Rioch equalised again to bring the score to 2–2.

With three minutes left it looked like a replay was in the offing, until a moment of high drama and controversy changed the complexion of the game. Everton's Ronnie Goodlass received the ball on the left and swung in a cross. McKenzie helped it on and from just six yards out Bryan Hamilton bundled the ball into the net past Ray Clemence.

Everyone in the ground, including the Liverpool players, thought it was a goal. Everyone, that is, except referee Clive Thomas, who awarded a free-kick against Hamilton.

Was it handball? Replays suggested Hamilton controlled the ball with his hip. Offside? When McKenzie played the ball through, Hamilton was fractionally behind Joey Jones, the last Liverpool defender.

Thomas would only say that he had spotted an infringement. But Everton's chance had gone and in the replay they were rolled over 3–0.

It was not the first time Hamilton had endured last-four heartache. Two years earlier, in a semi-final replay for Ipswich against West Ham, he had two goals disallowed. Again, the referee was Clive Thomas.

Indeed, Thomas was a ref who courted controversy. In the 1978 World Cup he blew for half-time just as Brazil were about to score from a corner, and in the League Cup final of 1981 he allowed Alan Kennedy of Liverpool to score, even though his team-mate Sammy Lee was prostrate in the box in front of West Ham 'keeper Phil Parkes.

— THE OVAL WINNERS —

For the first 21 years of its existence, the FA Cup final was played at Kennington Oval. In that time, entries increased from 15 to 163, and attendances from 2,000 in 1872 to 25,000 in 1892.

The winners during the Oval years were:

> Wanderers (5 wins)
> Blackburn Rovers (5)
> Old Etonians (2)
> West Bromwich Albion (2)
> Old Carthusians
> Oxford University
> Clapham Rovers
> Royal Engineers
> Blackburn Olympic
> Preston North End
> Aston Villa

— WAR STOPS PLAY – EVENTUALLY —

As if to emphasise their belief that it would all be over by Christmas, when World War One broke out in August 1914 the FA, in their wisdom, decided that the Cup should continue as normal.

Although strongly condemned, the competition was played throughout the winter, the only concession to the war effort being that replays now took place on Saturdays rather than midweek, and extra time was played wherever possible.

Nevertheless the final, on 24 April 1915, was a sombre affair in which Chelsea beat Sheffield United 3–0. Indeed, because Crystal Palace was being used as a war depot, the match was played at Old Trafford, and it became known as 'The Khaki Final' because of the huge number of servicemen among the 49,000 crowd.

As he handed the trophy to the winning skipper, Lord Derby hinted that this would be the last final for the foreseeable future, when he told the teams: 'You have played with one another and against one another for the Cup; play with one another for England now.'

— BURNLEY LANDMARK —

Jimmy Robson's goal for Burnley in 1962 was the 100th scored in nearly 40 years of Wembley Cup finals. The feat may well have achieved greater appreciation had it not been for the three that Tottenham bagged that day to secure the trophy for a second successive year.

— A H CHEQUER —

Morton Peto Betts, the scorer of the first FA Cup final goal, was down on the Wanderers' team sheet as A H Chequer. The reason? In the first round, Wanderers had been drawn against Harrow Chequers. The Chequers, unable to get a team together, scratched from the tournament and Betts (An Harrovian Chequer) was duly poached by Wanderers. This was in the days before players were cup-tied and was therefore all above board. Even if it wasn't, the man who signed Betts up was Wanderers captain Charles Alcock – who also happened to be secretary of the FA.

— NORTH–SOUTH DIVIDE: PART ONE —

'The northern contingent pay great attention to the matter of commissariat. They bring stone jars of strong ale and sandwiches an inch thick packed in little wicker baskets which are also used for conveying carrier pigeons. As a rule northerners and southerners, though they never fraternise, suffer each other gladly. Now and again there is an altercation when the expression of a London clerk, described as a "gormless gooby" by some Lancashire factory hand, is worth studying. The writer remembers a big Yorkshireman, accosted by a mechanical brain worker in a high stiff collar, hit off the other in the charming phrase "more clout nor pudding . . ." Assuredly every student of humanity will find much to interest him in the crowd of a Cup final.'

– Correspondent for the *London Evening News* in 1909.

— HAVE YOU SEEN THIS MAN? —

Nottingham Forest posted bills in Sheffield in 1883 offering a £20 reward for proof that one of Sheffield Wednesday's players was not properly qualified. Nobody came forward and the Owls exacted revenge by beating Forest 3–2 in a third-round replay.

— LEAGUE OF CUP FINALISTS —

Here's one for all the stats addicts – a league table of FA Cup finalists.
Two points have been awarded to winning teams, one to the losers.

Team	Finals	Pts
Arsenal	Won: 1930, 1936, 1950, 1971, 1979, 1993, 1998, 2002, 2003, 2005 Lost: 1927, 1932, 1952, 1972, 1978, 1980, 2001	29
Man Utd	Won: 1909, 1948, 1963, 1977, 1983, 1985, 1990, 1994, 1996, 1999, 2004 Lost: 1957, 1958, 1976, 1979, 1995, 2005	28
Newcastle	Won: 1910, 1924, 1932, 1951, 1952, 1955 Lost: 1905, 1906, 1908, 1911, 1974, 1998, 2001	19
Liverpool	Won: 1965, 1974, 1986, 1989, 1992, 2001 Lost: 1914, 1950, 1971, 1977, 1988, 1996	18
Everton	Won: 1906, 1933, 1966, 1984, 1995 Lost: 1893, 1897, 1907, 1968, 1985, 1986, 1989	17
Tottenham	Won: 1901, 1921, 1961, 1962, 1967, 1981, 1982, 1991 Lost: 1987	17
Aston Villa	Won: 1887, 1895, 1897, 1905, 1913, 1920, 1957 Lost: 1892, 1924, 2000	17
West Brom	Won: 1888, 1892, 1931, 1954, 1968 Lost: 1886, 1887, 1895, 1912, 1935	15
Blackburn	Won: 1884, 1885, 1886, 1890, 1891, 1928 Lost: 1882, 1960	14
Man City	Won: 1904, 1934, 1956, 1969 Lost: 1926, 1933, 1955, 1981	12
Wolves	Won: 1893, 1908, 1949, 1960 Lost: 1889, 1896, 1921, 1939	12
Bolton	Won: 1923, 1926, 1929, 1958 Lost: 1894, 1904, 1953	11
Sheffield Utd	Won: 1899, 1902, 1915, 1925 Lost: 1901, 1936	10
Wanderers	Won: 1872, 1873, 1876, 1877, 1878	10

Two points for winners, one for losing finalists

— SHIPSHAPE AND BRISTOL FASHION —

Leeds United stormed to the League Championship in 1974, and that season went 29 games unbeaten in the league. Predictably enough, their progress in the FA Cup was scuppered when they yet again came a cropper to lower-division opposition. The giant-killers on this occasion were Bristol City, languishing near the bottom of Division Two and widely tipped to be cannon fodder for Leeds when they met in the fifth round. The first game ended in a draw, but Leeds were confident of settling the tie in the replay at Elland Road. It was settled all right – by Bristol's Don Gillies, who fired past David Harvey in the 23rd minute for a famous win.

— BY 'ECK, WHO'S EMLEY? —

Situated midway between Huddersfield and Barnsley, Emley is the kind of nondescript West Yorkshire town that a stranger can pass through without ever knowing about it.

But in 1998, its Unibond League side put the town well and truly on the map with a stirring Cup run that had the whole nation taking notice.

They made their name by improbably surviving eight qualifying games before finally reaching the third round, where their opponents were Premiership outfit and two-time Cup winners West Ham United.

The game was played at Upton Park in front of 26,000 fans and when Frank Lampard put the Hammers ahead after four minutes it looked as if a rout was on the cards. But Emley rode their luck in spectacular fashion and in the second half, playing with a strong wind at their backs, scrambled an equaliser when David headed home from a corner.

Up against it, West Ham now took their turn to hang on, and had it not been for some bad luck and inexperience up front Emley might well have snatched an amazing victory.

With nine minutes remaining, however, the Hammers broke clear and a Stan Lazaridis cross was met by John Hartson for the decisive goal.

'By 'eck, who's Emley?' was the slogan written on midfielder Mark Wilson's T-shirt, and after the game everyone knew exactly who the plucky part-timers were.

— FIVE-MEDAL HAUL —

James Forrest played in all five of Blackburn Rovers' victorious finals up to 1891, and therefore is the last man to have collected five winner's medals. The other two were Arthur Kinnaird of Wanderers and Old Etonians, and Charles Wollaston of Wanderers. Forrest's other claim to fame was that he was the first professional to play for England. This illustrious band would have been joined by Manchester United's Roy Keane had his side not been pipped in a penalty shoot-out by Arsenal in 2005.

— IT TAKES ALLSORTS —

'And I honestly believe we can go all the way to Wembley . . . unless somebody knocks us out.'
– Dave 'Harry' Bassett.

— WEMBLEY: WHAT A LOAD OF RUBBISH! —

Such is the reverence with which Wembley Stadium is now held in FA Cup lore, it is strange to think that in its early years many seasoned observers blamed the stadium for a succession of distinctly ordinary finals.

In 1949 football writer Geoffrey Green was in no doubt as to the problem. 'That immaculate stretch of Wembley turf . . . its rich, thick surface being something not to be found by April on any club enclosure in the country, and this means that many a ground pass is not given sufficient bite, and falls short of its objective. The proportions of the huge stadium are another [problem], making distances so difficult to judge in the opening phases. These kinds of factors can lead to a loss of confidence which is not easy to restore.'

— HAT-TRICK KING —

Robert Earnshaw, who was playing for West Bromwich Albion in 2004–05, is the only player to have scored hat-tricks in the FA Cup, League Cup, Premiership, and Divisions One, Two and Three.

— THE RONNIE AND RICKY SHOW —

Just as Leeds had come a cropper to lowly opposition in 1971, so even greater indignity was heaped upon mighty Newcastle United in 1972. The Geordies were six-times winners of the Cup, in the top half of the First Division, and boasting the most exciting striker in the League in Malcolm Macdonald, so it seemed inconceivable that they would be turned over by Hereford United of the Southern League in the third round.

But not only did Newcastle fail to win, they failed to win twice. Those who remember the dramatic scenes at mud-soaked Edgar Street often forget that the first game between the two sides had been at St James's Park and produced an arguably bigger upset as the non-Leaguers came away with a 2–2 draw.

Normal service seemed to have been resumed in the replay as Macdonald pounced to give Newcastle the lead. But then up stepped Hereford's Ronnie Radford, skating over the mud before blasting an unstoppable shot from 30 yards past Willie McFaul.

As the game went into injury time, substitute Ricky George fired home the dramatic winner from eight yards, prompting a memorable pitch invasion by hundreds of youngsters in 'Snorkel' jackets and flares.

Up in the commentary box, a rookie BBC TV commentator called John Motson could hardly believe his luck that his first big game had turned out to be one of the biggest shocks in FA Cup history.

— WHO NEEDS THE MAGIC SPONGE? —

In the days before heat spray, ultrasound treatment and substitutes, Wigan Athletic turned to drastic measures to ensure star striker Harry Lyon could continue after being injured midway through a tense first-round replay against Doncaster Rovers in November 1965. Lyon, in agony after twisting his ankle, was carried to the dressing room where he was plied with whisky and painkillers. Despite being half-cut and perhaps spaced out by his drugs, Lyon returned to the fray, where he duly rattled in a hat-trick, including two strikes despatched with his injured foot.

— THE LONG AND THE SHORT OF IT —

Charlie Roberts was an uncompromising stopper and the rock of the Cup-winning Manchester United side at the turn of the 20th century. But he was also something of a dandy. In an era when footballers routinely wore their shorts down below the knee, Roberts caused a sensation when he turned out in a pair which daringly went down to the mid-thigh. The FA were less than impressed with his fashion sense and issued a decree that 'footballers' knickers must cover the knee'.

— DOUBLE WINNERS —

In all the League and FA Cup double has been achieved eight times. The full list of double winners is:

1889	Preston North End
1895	Aston Villa
1961	Tottenham Hotspur
1971	Arsenal
1986	Liverpool
1994	Manchester United
1996	Manchester United
1998	Arsenal
1999	Manchester United
2002	Arsenal

— THE JOY OF BEING A REF —

'Being chosen to referee the FA Cup final is the highest accolade any referee can receive. It means they think you are the best. In previous years the FA Cup final used to be given to the senior man on the list who was about to retire. It was a reward for services rendered. But the Football Association realised that this might not have been the correct way to go about things. My reward was 15 guineas and a medal. Not long before it was a fee *or* a medal. Everyone chose the gold medal.'
– Norman Burtenshaw, referee in the 1971 FA Cup final between Arsenal and Liverpool.

— WORDS OF WISDOM —

'With the Cup, the winners can laugh and the losers make their own arrangements.'
– Kevin Keegan.

— CONTROVERSIAL GLORY —

Newcastle United's Cup final replay win against Barnsley in 1910 was the first time the Magpies had won the trophy in four times of asking. But their glory was clouded with controversy. They were fined in an earlier round for fielding an under-strength team and censured by the FA for their handling of Cup final tickets. They even earned the soubriquet 'Dirty Newcastle' from the Barnsley fans for their robust tactics. Not that the Geordies were bothered – they were welcomed home as heroes and travelled through the streets of Newcastle in a convoy of eight open-topped landaus!

— THE MAN WHO SAVED SIR ALEX —

Lee Martin was a 23-year-old Manchester United defender who was not renowned for scoring goals. Indeed, his winner against Crystal Palace in the replay of the 1990 Cup final was his only goal that season. As far as his manager was concerned, however, it was possibly the most important goal of his career.

After a dismal season, Alex Ferguson was widely tipped for the sack if his under-achievers didn't beat unfancied Palace, and their failure to win the first match, drawn 3–3, only turned the screw further.

Martin's unexpected goal not only brought the silverware home to Old Trafford – but most probably saved Ferguson's job. Since then, the United boss hasn't done too badly . . .

— MOTTY'S MIKE RECORD —

When commentating for BBC TV on the 2003 Millennium showdown between Arsenal and Southampton, an enthusiastic fellow name of John Motson achieved an FA Cup record of his own. It was his 24th final appearance behind the mike, surpassing the previous record held by the legendary Kenneth 'They Think It's All Over' Wolstenholme.

— UNDER THE HAMMER —

The market for football memorabilia has never been so buoyant, and in May 2005 the greatest prize of all – the solid silver FA Cup used between 1896 and 1909 – provoked frenzied bidding when it came up for auction at Christie's in London. The trophy, presented to Lord Kinnaird as a souvenir of his long presidency of the Football Association, was eventually bought for a staggering £478,400 by David Gold, chairman of Birmingham City, who later donated it to the National Football Museum.

Other items of FA Cup memorabilia which went under the hammer in the same auction included:

- **£21,000**: A 1953 FA Cup winner's medal belonging to Blackpool's Stan Mortensen, a rare memento from the famous 'Matthews Final'.

- **£11,400**: A 1952 Arsenal Cup final shirt, numbered five with button-up collar, worn by Ray Daniels in the 1–0 defeat by Newcastle United.

- **£10,800**: Winner's medal awarded to George Stacey in 1909 after Manchester United's first win, 1–0 against Bristol City.

- **£8,400**: Stacey's 1909 white-and-red Manchester United shirt with lace-up collar and areas of staining.

- **£4,200**: Lee Martin's 1990 Manchester United Cup final shirt. Martin scored the winner in the replay against Crystal Palace.

- **£600**: Card from Arsenal's 1950 Cup celebration dinner held at the Café Royal.

- **£600**: Menu from Manchester United's 1957 post-game dinner at the Savoy.

- **£540**: Arsenal shirt worn by Freddie Ljungberg, a scorer in the 2002 final.

- **£360**: Arsenal versus Sheffield United 1936 Cup final match programme.

— PLAY IT AGAIN —

Every year on Cup final day, fans of Newcastle United and Bradford City play a re-enactment of the 1911 final between the two clubs, which ended with a controversial 1–0 replay win for the Yorkshiremen. Both sides dress up in replica kits and use a genuine 1911 ball.

— IF IT'S WEDNESDAY IT MUST BE WEMBLEY —

Reaching Wembley for the FA Cup final was once the pinnacle of a footballer's career. But in 1993, Arsenal and Sheffield Wednesday each played at the famous old stadium no fewer than four times in six weeks: FA Cup semi-final, League Cup final, FA Cup final and replay. Arsenal won both trophies, the first time a team had lifted both FA and League Cups in the same season.

— PRACTICE MAKES PERFECT —

The day before the 1988 FA Cup final, Wimbledon boss Bobby Gould instructed Alan Cork and Dennis Wise to hit some practice penalties at goalkeeper Dave Beasant. The cunning Gould had been watching Liverpool's spot-kick king John Aldridge during the season and noted that he usually put the ball low and to the goalkeeper's left. Sure enough, when Aldridge stepped up to take Liverpool's 61st-minute penalty in an attempt to level the final, he placed it low and to the left – where it was saved by Beasant.

— THE START OF SOMETHING BIG —

On 3 January 1975 Nottingham Forest were a nondescript Second Division outfit, and few outside the city noticed when, on the eve of their third-round tie against Tottenham Hotspur, manager Allan Brown was sacked. Somehow Forest managed a draw, and three days later the club announced their new appointment: Brian Clough. The impact of 'Old Big 'Ead' was immediate. On 8 January a Neil Martin goal gave Forest victory in the replay and so began an era of unprecedented success at the City Ground, culminating within four years with League Championship and European Cup triumphs.

— MONTY'S DOUBLE SAVE —

At full-time at the end of Sunderland's astounding 1973 Cup final win over Leeds United, it was not winning goal-scorer Ian Porterfield who was embraced by manager Bob Stokoe, but goalkeeper Jim Montgomery, whose heroic double save had kept the Second Division side in the game at a crucial time.

• First, Montgomery sprawls to his left to save Trevor Cherry's six-yard diving header.

• Still on the floor, Monty raises his hands to somehow parry Peter Lorimer's close-range follow-up on to the crossbar.

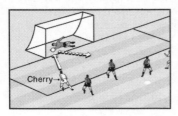 

— MAKE YOUR MIND UP, SPURS! —

When Tottenham won the FA Cup in 1901, they were wearing their now-traditional white shirts and navy-blue shorts. But the colour scheme was far from traditional back then. Formed less than ten years earlier, the Spurs had experimented with all navy, blue-and-white halves, red shirts and blue shorts, and even chocolate and gold.

— THE MIGHTY BLACKBURN —

'The prowess of the early "Blues and Whites" is still the subject of conversation in sporting circles all over the world. In the back blocks of the Antipodes, on the Canadian prairies, and in far-away China and Japan their stirring deeds on the football field are discussed as eagerly as in factories, shops, and offices in the homeland.'
– Charles Francis, *The History of the Blackburn Rovers Football Club* (1925).

— MANCHESTER DISUNITED —

When Manchester United were invited to take part in the FIFA World Club Championship in 1999–2000 – a tournament which clashed with the third round of the FA Cup – nobody was particularly bothered because nobody seriously expected the club to go.

The fact that United withdrew from the Cup and jetted out to Rio instead shocked everyone except the marketing men who made it happen.

The Reds were soon on their way back after being dumped out of the new competition in the early rounds, but the damage was done. Not only had they devalued the most famous of all football competitions, but the ill-advised trip was a sad victory for the powers of money and marketing over more than 120 years of FA Cup tradition.

— THE WORLD CUP —

The 1997 FA Cup final between Middlesbrough and Chelsea must rank as the competition's most cosmopolitan. In all, it featured five Italians (Di Matteo, Zola, Vialli, Festa and Ravanelli), two Brazilians (Juninho, Emerson), a Frenchman (Lebocuf), a Dane (Beck), a Slovak (Kinder), a Romanian (Petrescu) and a Norwegian (Grodas). Chelsea were managed by a Dutchman, Ruud Gullit – the first non-British manager to guide a side to victory in the Cup final.

— WATFORD WALLOPED —

In the first round of the 1911–12 FA Cup, little Watford surprised everyone by managing a goalless draw at home to the powerful Wolves, and came close to claiming the Midlanders' scalp on several occasions. As a result, they arrived at Molineux for the replay sensing an opportunity for an epoch-making act of giant-killing. Sadly, on this occasion, the magic of the Cup was nowhere to be seen. Wolves pulverised them 10–0.

— GREEN IS THE COLOUR! —

Long before the free-spending era of Roman Abramovich, Chelsea were just like any other club, trying to make an honest bob or two to keep their heads above water. Presumably this is why the Blues came up with the ingenious idea of charging fans £15 a time to be photographed beside the FA Cup which they had won in 1997. With more than a thousand takers every month, it proved to be a remarkably lucrative venture and netted the club £180,000 during the year the trophy was in their possession at Stamford Bridge.

— NON-LEAGUERS WIN THEIR SPURS —

The huge crowd of 110,820 for the 1901 final included 40,000 who had made the long trek south from Yorkshire, and all of them must have been expecting a rout when mighty Sheffield United, including nine internationals, turned out against non-League no-hopers Tottenham Hotspur at Crystal Palace.

Astonishingly, United only just managed to scrape a 2–2 draw, courtesy of a highly dodgy goal awarded by referee Arthur Kingscott.

Even more amazingly, the replay at Bolton's Burnden Park ended with Spurs running out convincing 3–1 winners, thereby becoming the first – and only – non-League winners of the FA Cup.

— LOSERS BECOME WINNERS —

In 1992 a new innovation was introduced to Cup final protocol. Instead of the losers waiting disconsolately for the winners to receive the trophy before climbing the famous 39 steps to collect their medals, it was decided they would go first.

Sunderland, having been beaten 2–0 by Liverpool, duly trudged up to the royal box where they were, inevitably, presented with winners' medals by mistake. It was not until Liverpool had lifted the Cup that the error was rectified back on the pitch.

— MATCH OF THE DAY —

For the first year of its existence, BBC's flagship football show *Match of the Day* was restricted to showing League matches only. In 1966, however, the cameras were at Anfield for the third-round clash between Liverpool and Chelsea. In grainy black-and-white, Liverpool's Roger Hunt – who had netted *MOTD*'s first ever goal the previous season – scored again, but goals by Peter Osgood and Bobby Tambling were enough to silence the Kop and send Chelsea into the next round.

— NORTH–SOUTH DIVIDE: PART TWO —

'London witnessed an incursion of Northern barbarians, hot-blooded Lancastrians, sharp of tongue, rough and ready, of uncouth garb and speech. A tribe of Soudanese Arabs let loose in the Strand would not excite more amusement and curiosity. Strange oaths fell upon Southern ears.'
– Excerpt from the *Pall Mall Gazette*, after Blackburn Rovers fans descended on the capital for the 1884 Cup final.

— ALL IN FOR THE CUP —

In a move eerily prescient of modern-day attempts to form super-leagues and elite cup competitions, in 1919 the Football League put forward a plan to kill off the qualifying rounds for non-League teams and restrict the FA Cup to just 64 Football League clubs. Happy to report, the Football Association took the view that a restricted tournament would seriously infringe the rights of hundreds of smaller clubs, and thereby kept the magic of this unique competition alive to the present day.

— FA CUP MASTERMIND —

In the 1970s and '80s, *FA Cup Mastermind*, featuring a host of celebrities and old footballers, was a staple of Cup final day TV coverage. But barrister Shaun Wallace took the concept a stage further in 2004 when he won the real *Mastermind* series answering questions on 'FA Cup Finals since 1970' as his specialist subject.

— THE HAMMERS HAVE A BALL —

In 1975 the solemnity of the fourth-round draw was shattered when one of the FA Cup officials withdrew West Ham's ball from the velvet bag – and dropped it on the floor. After a few frantic moments the ball was recovered. But instead of being paired with Leeds United, as the Londoners should have been, the ball was placed back in the bag. New opponents for Leeds were drawn and the Hammers ended up with a home tie instead. That year they went on to win the Cup.

— THE NEWCASTLE HOODOO —

Between 1905 and 1911 Newcastle United were undisputed Cup final kings. They appeared in five finals in seven years at the Crystal Palace stadium yet, remarkably, they won only one, when they beat Barnsley 2–0 after a replay. After losing for a third time in succession United skipper Colin Veitch suggested that the FA buy a new Cup so that his side might have a chance of winning it!

The Geordies' results during that amazing period were:

1905:	Lost	Newcastle 0, Aston Villa 2
1906:	Lost	Newcastle 0, Everton 1
1907:	Lost	– in the first round to Crystal Palace
1908:	Lost	Newcastle 1, Wolverhampton Wanderers 3
1909:	Lost	– in the semi-final to Manchester United
1910:	Won	Newcastle 1, Barnsley 1
		replay Newcastle 2, Barnsley 0
1911:	Lost	Newcastle 0, Bradford City 1

— BRADFORD BEAT THE BUG —

A flu epidemic at Bradford in 1976 forced their fifth-round encounter with Norwich City to be postponed twice. For the third date, the Fourth Division outfit rose, Lazarus-like, from their sickbeds and recorded one of the great giant-killing acts by beating the Canaries – who were flying high in Division One – by a goal to nil. The win meant that the Yorkshiremen became only the third team from the basement division to reach the quarter-finals, where they were beaten by the eventual Cup winners, Southampton.

— THE LEATHERHEAD LIP —

It was 1975. Another year, and another name to feature on the FA Cup's roster of gallant non-League sides responsible for scaring the living daylights out of football's aristocrats.

On this occasion the part-timers were Leatherhead of the Isthmian League, who that term were one of five clubs from outside the League to reach the fourth round. Their reward was a plum home tie against Division One Leicester City, a game which was controversially switched to Filbert Street because of the limitations of the Fetcham Grove ground.

After 27 minutes, home advantage did not seem to matter as first Peter McGillicuddy and then Chris Kelly – known as 'The Leatherhead Lip' for his outspoken comments – found the net to give their team a shock 2–0 lead.

Early in the second half, it might well have been all over. Kelly broke clear, rounded Mark Wallington in the Leicester goal, but saw his shot agonisingly hooked clear off the line by Malcolm Munro.

The save was to prove the turning point in the game. Jon Sammels and Steve Earle drew Leicester level before Keith Weller pounced to score a late winner.

It was a bitter disappointment for Leatherhead, who at the very least deserved a lucrative replay. For the lippy Kelly, however, there was a silver lining as he went on to sign a full-time contract with Millwall.

— WORLD-FAMOUS WIN —

A week after non-League Sutton United famously toppled Coventry City of the First Division in 1989, they received a newspaper clipping about their triumph – from a publication in South China.

— A CREDIT TO MERSEYSIDE —

'Ladies and gentlemen, yesterday at Wembley we might have lost the Cup but you the Liverpool people have won everything. You have won the admiration of the policemen in London and you have won the admiration of the public in London.'
– Bill Shankly after losing the FA Cup in 1971 to Arsenal.

— A TALE OF THREE GOALKEEPERS —

Leicester City beat fellow Second Division side Shrewsbury 5–2 to progress to the semi-finals of the FA Cup in 1982, but the victory was anything but routine for the Foxes.

With the scores locked at 1–1, 'keeper Mark Wallington injured himself in a collision with Shrewsbury's Chic Bates. Although he manfully stayed on the pitch, when Jack Keay made it 2–1 to Town it was clear that Wallington could not continue. Without a replacement goalkeeper on the bench, Leicester boss Jock Wallace was forced to hand the green jersey to striker Alan Young.

The gangling Young made a series of vital saves as his side got back level, but then disaster struck when he knocked himself senseless in a collision with Keay. There was nothing the bemused Wallace could do except put winger Steve Lynex in goal until Young's head cleared.

For ten long minutes the Shrews attacked desperately, only for Lynex to deny them. Then, when Young returned, Lynex moved forward again and carved out a chance for Melrose to score Leicester's third. Dumbfounded, Shrewsbury conceded two more in a game that would be remembered by trivia buffs as one in which seven goals were scored but two goalkeepers kept clean sheets!

— BATTLING BARNSLEY—

In 1911–12 Barnsley played six goalless games in an extraordinary Cup campaign that saw them reach the final for the second time in three years, a record for a Second Division club. In all they played 12 matches, of which three went to extra time. One of these was the final, which was a turgid 0–0 draw against West Bromwich Albion. The Yorkshiremen won the replay 1–0.

— DISOBEYING ORDERS —

'You must be joking, Skip.'
– Arsenal centre-half Leslie Compton's response to his captain Joe Mercer's instructions not to go upfield for a last-gasp corner in the 1950 semi-final against Chelsea. Compton duly scored from his brother Denis's inswinger and made the score 2–2. Arsenal went on to win the replay and the Cup.

— A PINT TO PREPARE —

Wimbledon were never the most orthodox of teams, and on the eve of the 1988 FA Cup final, while their opponents Liverpool were tucked up in bed, the Crazy Gang decided to descend en masse on the local pub for a few pre-match beers. Alan Cork, a veteran who had played for the Dons since the early days in the lower leagues, had rather too much to drink. Suffering from a pounding hangover, he was forced to wear sunglasses as he travelled to Wembley the next morning.

— G FOR GINGER —

In the days when they were known as the Throstles rather than the Baggies, West Bromwich Albion enjoyed a great deal of FA Cup success. In 1931, as a Second Division side, they won the trophy by beating Birmingham 2–1. Scorer of both goals that day was W G Richardson. The redhead had adopted the middle name Ginger to distinguish himself from his team-mate W Richardson, who played in defence.

— CUP OF CHEER —

After the Cup was stolen in 1895, the FA quickly ordered a replacement. Unfortunately, they forgot to copyright the design – with the result that within a few years even the winners of park competitions were being handed copies of the hallowed trophy.

In 1910, the FA decided enough was enough and 'retired' the Cup. A sum of 50 guineas was set aside and an invitation sent out to silversmiths to come up with a design for the new pot. The winners were a Bradford firm called Fattorini & Sons, and their handsome new design took pride of place at the 1911 Cup final. Ironically, the match was won by . . . Bradford City.

— TEAM CONSISTENCY —

When Bolton won the FA Cup in 1923, 1926 and 1929 they completed their hat-trick by using a total of 17 players.

— THE MATTHEWS FINAL —

At the age of 38, Stanley Matthews was a national institution who had achieved so much in the domestic game, but had never collected an FA Cup winner's medal. Indeed, having tried and failed in the finals of 1948 and 1951, it seemed 'The King of Soccer' was destined never to get his hands on the world's most famous trophy.

In 1953, Matthews and his beloved Blackpool found themselves back at Wembley for their third final in five years. The opposition were Bolton, and while the nation united behind Matthews, the hard men from Burnden Park showed little such sentiment. They were ahead within 75 seconds, led 2–1 at the interval and with ten minutes to go Eric Bell had put them 3–1 ahead.

But if defeat was staring Blackpool in the face, Matthews had different ideas. First a mesmerising run resulted in a cross which Stan Mortensen bundled home. And when Mortensen thumped in a free-kick to level the scores with three minutes left, the stage was set for 'The Wizard of Dribble' to take a bow.

A minute of injury time had already passed when Matthews received the ball in his customary position on the right wing. Hugging the touchline, the ball seemingly glued to his feet, he danced around Bolton left-back Ralph Banks and delivered an inch-perfect cross along the deck for Bill Perry to smack into the back of the net.

It didn't matter that Mortensen had scored three, or that Perry had bagged the winner. The day – and the Cup – belonged at last to Stanley Matthews.

— HE AIN'T HEAVY, HE'S LORD KINNAIRD —

Travelling to the 1873 Cup final, in which he was due to play for Wanderers against Oxford University, Lord Kinnaird found his carriage being mobbed by several dozen adoring fans. The supporters unhitched the horses and pulled the carriage all the way to the Oval. Kinnaird repaid their devotion by scoring one of Wanderers' two goals as they won for the second year running.

— STOKES – ONE NIL! —

Mayday 1976: with a combination of unknowns, journeymen and wily old foxes in their line-up, Second Division Southampton held off the young Turks of Manchester United for 83 minutes before unleashing the killer blow and winning the Cup.

The goal was scored by Bobby Stokes, a loyal Saint who played more than 200 games for the club between 1968 and 1977. A legend in Southampton, Stokes sadly died of natural causes in 1995.

• Just inside his own half, Jim McCalliog plays the ball behind a static United back four. Stokes is on to it in a flash, beating the offside trap and leaving Martin Buchan for dead.

• From 25 yards out Stokes fires into the corner of the net past the despairing grasp of Alex Stepney, who had come out to narrow the angle.

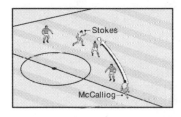 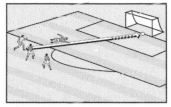

— CUTLER HITS THE BACK OF THE NET —

In 1957 Reg Cutler of Bournemouth had the Wolverhampton Wanderers crowd in hysterics when, while running in on goal, he sprinted instead into the netting, broke one of the posts, and was tangled up like a fish. Cutler had the last laugh, however. He scored the winner which knocked highly fancied Wolves out of the Cup at the fourth-round stage, causing one of the major upsets of that year's competition.

— A ROYAL FIRST —

Burnley had just beaten Liverpool 1–0 in the 1914 Cup final and for skipper Tommy Boyle there was an extra treat in store. He was the first captain to receive the FA Cup from a reigning monarch. King George V sported a red rose to celebrate the all-Lancashire occasion.

— A TALE OF TWO ST JAMES'S PARKS —

Having toppled First Division Leicester in the fourth round, Exeter City arrived at St James's Park, Newcastle, in the unusual position of not quite being rank outsiders. It was 1981, a year before Kevin Keegan's arrival electrified Tyneside, and the Magpies were in the doldrums of the Second Division. Exeter were in the division below, but their startling 3–1 win over the Foxes at their own St James Park ground sent them into the uncharted waters of the last 16 on the crest of a wave.

On paper things looked grim for the men from Devon when Alan Shoulder gave United the lead after 57 minutes, but in reality Exeter were bossing the game and it was no surprise when, with four minutes remaining, Lee Roberts toe-poked the ball into the net for the equaliser. So it was that the action switched to St James Park 350 miles to the south, and it was here, in front of a crowd of almost 18,000, that Exeter inflicted yet more FA Cup humiliation on hapless Newcastle.

Even the 4–0 scoreline does not do justice to the way in which Exeter annihilated the Geordies. It was a turkey shoot, and by the end of the 90 minutes the visitors were utterly destroyed.

In the quarter-finals, the Grecians found themselves at White Hart Lane, where they gallantly succumbed 2–0 to the eventual Cup winners, Tottenham. But by then Exeter had already written a chapter for themselves in the book of giant-killing legend.

— IT'S THAT MAN AGAIN —

Even when their playing careers were ended, the original 'Gang of Seven' who dreamed up the FA Cup in 1871 found it hard to step away from their creation. Major Francis Marindin, who captained Royal Engineers in the first-ever final, refereed no fewer than eight consecutive finals between 1882 and 1990.

— SWINDON GIANT-KILLERS —

Swindon Town never reached the rarefied heights of the old First Division, but they had no problem disposing of so-called superior opposition. Between their first Cup game in 1907 and their 100th in the competition in 1981, they knocked out no fewer than 16 top-flight opponents.

— GOALS – BUT NO GLORY —

The Manchester City side of 1925–26 could not stop scoring goals, bagging more than 100 in both League and Cup that season. Sadly, they couldn't stop letting them in, either. Their shaky defence cost them dear in a tense FA Cup final, when they lost to Bolton by a single goal. Eight days later, needing only a point to stay up, they were beaten 3–2 by Notts County and therefore became the first side to get to Wembley and be relegated in the same season.

— CUP CALAMITY —

When Liverpool skipper Mark Wright lifted the FA Cup after beating Sunderland 2–0 in 1992, he was, in fact, hoisting an exact replica of the original trophy which had become too fragile to sustain another day of being thrown about on the pitch.

Just as well. While putting the new trophy on the team bus, Liverpool's jubilant players succeeded in denting it. The following week the Cup was back at the silversmiths for intensive repairs.

— THOSE WERE THE DAYS —

'The Crystal Palace was more than the venue of a football match; it took on the character of a picnic. Long before the game happy parties sat in groups, under the trees, munching sandwiches, and generations of football folk met there to renew old acquaintances.'
– William Pickford (FA Council member 1888–1937) in *A Few Recollections of Sport* (1939).

— A CUP TREBLE —

When Jimmy Delaney pocketed an Irish Cup winner's medal with Derry City in 1954, it was the final piece of silverware in a unique treble for the former Scottish international winger. In 1937 Delaney was part of the Celtic team which won the Scottish Cup, and 11 years later he helped Manchester United lift the FA Cup at Wembley.

— POWER STRUGGLES —

The relationship between the Football Association and the Football League has never been smooth, and in 1973 it erupted into full-scale warfare in which the very future of the FA Cup was placed in jeopardy.

The row was over television fees, and at one point matters became so fractious a special meeting of the League clubs came within a whisker of boycotting the competition.

'I can't imagine a bigger or more important story than our clubs refusing to play in the Cup,' said League secretary Alan Hardaker. 'It would affect millions of people and cost the game millions of pounds. But nobody, in their hearts, wants to harm the Cup.'

A few years later a suggestion that the FA should pay for the privilege of having League clubs in the tournament led to renewed open warfare and threats of the Cup being cancelled. But once again sentimentality won the day over pragmatism and the clubs stopped short of bringing the grand old competition to a juddering halt.

— DERBY ARE BURIED —

Cup kings in 1903 were little Bury, who thrashed much-fancied Derby County 6–0 in the final – the highest winning margin in Cup final history. But having overcome the likes of Wolves, Sheffield United, Notts County and Aston Villa on the way without conceding a goal, the Lancastrian minnows' name was well and truly written on the trophy from the start.

— WELSH RAREBIT —

Welsh international goalkeeper Dan Lewis was the toast of the Valleys in 1927 as Cardiff became the first and last non-English team to lift the FA Cup. Unfortunately for Lewis, he was in goal for Arsenal at the time. It was his ghastly error, allowing a soft shot from Hugh Ferguson to squirm through his hands, which presented the Bluebirds with the winning goal in the 73rd minute.

— WILLIE YOUNG'S TACKLE —

Arsenal's Willie Young was a no-nonsense centre-half who had little time for the romance of the FA Cup. In 1980, while everyone in the land was talking about 17-year-old West Ham midfielder Paul Allen becoming the youngest player to appear in a Wembley FA Cup final, Young's only concern was making sure that the kid was on the losing side.

The Arsenal stopper's mood cannot have been sweet as his team conceded an early goal to, of all unlikely events, a Trevor Brooking header, and then proceeded to play the rest of the match like headless chickens. Deep into the second half, Young got his chance to vent his frustrations – and the unfortunate victim was Paul Allen.

Set clear by an incisive through-ball which splintered Arsenal's ragged back four, Allen hared towards Pat Jennings' goal and seemed odds-on to become Wembley's youngest scorer until Young, labouring in his wake, scythed him down from behind.

Today, of course, the tackle would have merited an immediate red card – and even in 1980 Young should have been given his marching orders.

Inexplicably, referee Graeme Courtney decided to merely book Young and award a free-kick, which was subsequently squandered. The Hammers hung on to win, but had it not been for Young's cynical tackle their victory might have been even sweeter in the Allen household.

— A WEEK IS A LONG TIME IN FOOTBALL —

Notts County must have felt supremely confident as they went into the 1891 Cup final against the mighty Blackburn Rovers. After all, only a week earlier they had trounced the Lancashire club 7–1 in a League match. Blackburn, however, had played an under-strength team in the first encounter and in the final normal service was resumed as they convincingly beat County 3–1.

— BOMBED OUT —

In 1946 Hull City were prevented from entering the FA Cup because of bomb damage to their ground.

— CAPTAINS UNITED —

To celebrate the 100th FA Cup final in 1981, 30 Cup-winning captains were paraded in front of the crowd. To get them there was no mean feat. David Barber of the FA took more than a month to track them all down. They were:

Danny Blanchflower (Tottenham Hotspur, 1961 and 1962)
Tony Book (Manchester City, 1969)
Jack Burkitt (Nottingham Forest, 1959)
Noel Cantwell (Manchester United, 1963)
Johnny Carey (Manchester United, 1948)
Raich Carter (Sunderland, 1937)
Johnny Dixon (Aston Villa, 1957)
Joe Harvey (Newcastle United, 1951 and 1952)
Emlyn Hughes (Liverpool, 1974)
Bobby Kerr (Sunderland, 1973)
Brian Labone (Everton, 1966)
Nat Lofthouse (Bolton Wanderers, 1958)
Dave Mackay (Tottenham Hotspur, 1967)
Frank McLintock (Arsenal, 1971)
Joe Mercer (Arsenal, 1950)
Len Millard (West Bromwich Albion, 1954)
Mick Mills (Ipswich Town, 1978)
Bobby Moore (West Ham United, 1964)
Tom Parker (Arsenal, 1930)
Roy Paul (Manchester City, 1956)
Dick Pym (Bolton Wanderers, 1923, 1926 and 1929 – not captain, but at 88 one of the oldest surviving finalists at that time)
Pat Rice (Arsenal, 1979)
Peter Rodrigues (Southampton, 1976)
Jimmy Scoular (Newcastle United, 1955)
Bill Slater (Wolverhampton Wanderers, 1960)
Tom Smith (Preston North End, 1938)
Ronnie Starling (Sheffield Wednesday, 1935)
Jack Swann (Huddersfield Town, 1920 – not captain, but played in the first final after World War One)
Don Welsh (Charlton Athletic, 1947)
Graham Williams (West Bromwich Albion, 1968)
Billy Wright (Wolverhampton Wanderers, 1949)
Ron Yeats (Liverpool, 1965)

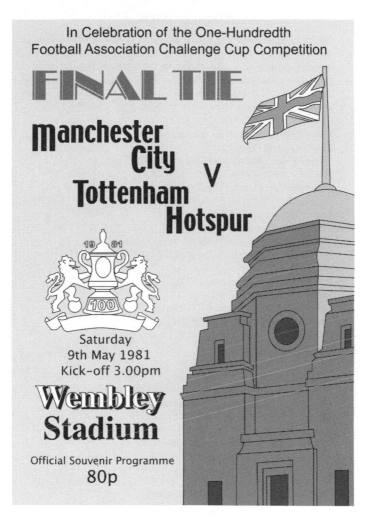

In Celebration of the One-Hundredth
Football Association Challenge Cup Competition

FINAL TIE

Manchester City v Tottenham Hotspur

Saturday
9th May 1981
Kick-off 3.00pm

Wembley Stadium

Official Souvenir Programme
80p

— NUMBERS GAME —

Numbers were first worn on players' shirts in a final
when Everton played Manchester City in 1933. Instead
of being numbered 1–11, both teams were collectively
numbered 1–22.

— EARLY KICK-OFF —

he Cup final is traditionally played in May, but the road to glory starts a full ten months earlier when the 600 or so non-League teams who enter the competition each year start to play their qualifying rounds. If one of them is lucky enough to reach the third round, they will have already played five ties – and will be just seven wins away from the final itself! The progress goes like this:

First Round (proper)
80 teams, made up of 48 from the Football League's two lower divisions, plus 32 survivors from the qualifying rounds.

Second Round
40 teams

Third Round
64 teams, made up of 44 from the Premiership and Championship, plus 20 survivors from the second round.

Fourth Round
32 teams

Fifth Round
16 teams

Sixth Round
8 teams

Semi-Final
4 teams

Final
2 teams

— LUCKY MASON? —

Eddie Mason was a member of the Dragoon Guards and a useful wing-half. During the Great War he fought at Marne, Ypres and Aisne and survived those terrible battles without a scratch. However, on his return in 1918 Mason was signed up by Hull City – and in his first game, a Cup qualifier, he was stretchered off with a broken leg.

— WALTHAMSTOW ON THE MARCH —

In 1953 amateur club Walthamstow Avenue beat two League opponents in the FA Cup before amazingly holding Manchester United to a 1–1 draw at Old Trafford in the fourth round. The replay was staged at Highbury, where the part-timers were not disgraced in a 5–2 defeat by the First Division side.

— MORE FAMOUS LAST WORDS —

'If they score now, I'll eat my hat!'
– BBC Radio commentator Commander Tom Woodroffe, seconds before Preston's George Mutch was felled in the box by Huddersfield's Alf Young for the penalty which gave the Lancastrians a 1–0 Cup final win in 1938.

— THE PHOENIX RISES —

Three months earlier the team had been decimated in the Munich air crash. Yet in May 1958 Manchester United made the FA Cup final, where they lost 2–0 to Bolton with a team containing only four of the original Busby Babes.

— WONDERFUL WYCOMBE —

As FA Cup glory runs go, few can compete with wonderful Wycombe Wanderers' 2000–01 campaign in which the side from the Third Division (the old Fourth) very nearly went all the way to Wembley.

Perhaps their success that year was down to the fact that they were managed by Lawrie Sanchez, the old warhorse whose goal had given Wimbledon their sensational 1988 Cup final win over Liverpool. Or perhaps it was the luck of the draw. Either way, Wycombe never looked back after beating Grimsby in the third round and reaching the fourth round for the first time in their 116-year history.

Ironically, after Lawrie's side had disposed of Wolves, it was Wimbledon who were next up in the fifth round. The Dons were on a slide which had already taken them out of the top flight, and their defeat to Wycombe in a replay penalty shoot-out was one of the final nails in their coffin.

Now Wycombe found themselves in the quarter-finals, where they were paired with Premiership side Leicester City. After another tenacious performance, the scores were level at 1–1 as the game went into stoppage time. With just seconds remaining, Wycombe were awarded a free-kick; the ball was swept into the box and there to stab it home was Roy Essendoh, a player who had only been signed by Sanchez after answering a job offer on Teletext.

Astonishingly, Wycombe were now in the semis. Their opponents were Liverpool, and more than 20,000 fans descended on Villa Park for the biggest game in the Wanderers' history. They were rewarded with a marvellously resolute performance which kept the Premiership side at bay until the 75th minute, when Emile Heskey powered Liverpool in front with a header. A few minutes later Robbie Fowler doubled the lead – but there was still time for one more moment of FA Cup glory. Receiving the ball on the edge of the box, Keith Ryan executed an exquisite chip into the Merseysiders' net, a finish which, although too late to change the outcome, sent Wycombe's army of fans into ecstasy.

Back home in Buckinghamshire, the team were welcomed as heroes, with an open-topped bus trip through the town and a civic reception held in their honour. For Sanchez it was a moment to compare with his 1988 triumph, and for FA Cup aficionados another entry in the long and illustrious legend of giant-killing greats.

— HOME FROM HOME —

In 1950 Arsenal won the Cup without leaving London. Drawn at home in the first four rounds, they were paired with Chelsea in the semi-final, which was played at Tottenham's White Hart Lane. In the final they travelled the short distance to Wembley and beat Liverpool 2–0, Reg Lewis getting both goals.

— THANKS, CHARLES —

In 1881 the undisputed 'Father of the FA Cup', Charles Alcock, was presented with a scroll 'in recognition of all that he has done during the past 18 years to establish and further the Association game'. He was also given a silver inkstand and a purse containing 300 guineas.

— GOALS ON BOTH SIDES —

The 1928 FA Cup final between Blackburn Rovers and Huddersfield Town was won 3–1 by the Lancastrians. Remarkably, it was the first time in 18 years that both teams had scored in the final.

— AN IN-HOUSE AFFAIR —

The seven-man Football Association committee which launched the first Challenge Cup competition in 1871 included the two captains of the first final, Charles Alcock of Wanderers and Capt. Francis Marindin of Royal Engineers; the scorer of the game's only goal, Morton Peto Betts; and the match referee, Alfred Stair.

— THE MAGNIFICENT KENYON-SLANEY —

One of the FA Cup's early greats was William Kenyon-Slaney, who helped Wanderers win the trophy in 1873 and then played for Old Etonians in the finals of 1875 and 1876. He also scored the first-ever international goal – for England against Scotland at the Oval in 1873.

— VARSITY NEAR-MISS —

Although Oxford and Cambridge Universities both competed in the first few FA Cup competitions, the two sides never played against each other in the final. The nearest they came was in 1877, when both sides reached the semi-finals. But while Oxford went through, Cambridge were ousted by the competition's eventual winners, Wanderers.

— A HANDSHAKE FOR BRAVE JONES —

Mick Jones provided the cross from which Allan 'Sniffer' Clarke scored the only goal of the centenary FA Cup final against Arsenal in 1972. In the process, Jones fell awkwardly and dislocated his shoulder. Despite this, he insisted on climbing the steps to the royal box to receive his medal – and a painful handshake – from the Queen.

— TROPHY-HUNTING TOFFEEMEN —

When it comes to the FA Cup, few teams have as much history with the old trophy as Everton. Not only have they won more FA Cup matches than any other club, they have played in more quarter-finals, more semi-finals, and progressed through more FA Cup rounds than any other club. Mind you, they have also lost seven finals – more than any other club.

— TICKET TOUT —

West Bromwich Albion's Jeff Astle was a hero after scoring the winner against Everton in the 1968 Cup final. But two years later he was fined £100 and stripped of the club captaincy after admitting in an interview that he had made a £200 profit flogging tickets for the Wembley clash.

— GOOD OLD GOODISON —

When the FA Cup final of 1894 was played at Everton's Goodison Park, it was the first time in the history of the competition that the climax had taken place on the ground of a football club.

— SIX OF THE BEST —

George Best was never a great respecter of authority, and at the end of the 1960s his errant behaviour meant that he spent more time on the front pages of the newspapers than the back. In January 1970 matters reached a head at Old Trafford when the mercurial Irishman had a post-match row with referee Jack Taylor and was suspended for a month. On 7 February, FA Cup fifth-round day, Best returned to the fray with a point to prove – and hapless Northampton Town were unlucky enough to be Manchester United's opponents.

Producing one of the finest displays of his illustrious career, Best mesmerised the Cobblers from the first whistle to the last, running through his extensive repertoire of trickery and scoring six sensational goals.

Like their team, the 22,000 partisan fans packed into Northampton's compact County Ground could only watch Best's single-handed destruction in awe. The match finished 8–2, with Brian Kidd helping himself to the Red Devils' other two goals, and Best's haul equalling the FA Cup scoring record.

Two years later, Best was at it again. On 8 January he went AWOL and, when he finally showed up two days later, United manager Frank O'Farrell fined him two weeks' wages, ordered the controversial star out of his luxury house and insisted he move into digs. He was also made to attend extra training sessions. On 19 January, Best returned to the side and put in another magnificent man-of-the-match performance as United beat Southampton 3–1 in the third round.

— NOT SO DAFT —

By 1894 the game had gone professional, but this did not mean that amateurism was totally extinct. Outside-left for Notts County was the brilliantly named Harry Daft. Unpaid, Daft scored 18 Cup goals for County as well as representing England five times and opening the batting for Nottinghamshire.

— THE AULD ENEMY —

Queen's Park from Glasgow were one of the few Scottish teams to take part in the FA Cup, being one of a small number able to afford the rail fare to London. Twice they reached the final and twice they were beaten by the 'auld enemy', losing to Blackburn Rovers in 1884 and 1885.

— SHEFFIELD UNITED —

While watching a semi-final at Bramall Lane cricket ground in Sheffield, several local dignitaries had a bright idea: why not form a football section of the Sheffield United Cricket Club? This they did in 1889 – with lasting results.

— DAPPER JACK —

Legendary Portsmouth boss Jack Tinn was a firm believer that wearing lucky white spats on match day would help his side to victory. He was not far wrong. In 1939 his side defeated all the odds to reach the FA Cup final, in which they outplayed red-hot favourites Wolves to record a sensational 4–1 win. Later that year war broke out, and Pompey held the trophy for six years.

—A FINAL AMONG FINALS —

'The finest heroes of all, and the most gripping, emotional final I have been to – and that includes the two in which I carried off the Cup.'
– Spurs legend Danny Blanchflower on Sunderland's 1973 Cup final win over Leeds United.

— WEATHER-ING THE STORM —

In 1987, with his car blocked in, Gillingham's never-say-die captain Mark Weather set off on foot through thick snow in order to play in his side's third-round tie against Wigan. Six exhausting miles later, the aptly named Weather arrived at the ground – only to discover that the match had been called off.

— KICK-AND-RUSH TACTICS —

Football was originally designed as a dribbling game, but Royal Engineers, with their belief in kick-and-rush tactics, were the Wimbledon of their day. In the 1878 Cup final against Wanderers, the Engineers got the ball on halfway, surrounded it in a pack and kept on running until they found themselves in the opposition goal. Because nobody was sure who had got the last touch, it is down in FA Cup final history as the only goal without a goal-scorer.

— MISTAKEN IDENTITY —

Having just scored the goal which secured Chelsea's 1970 replay win over Leeds United, David Webb was all too happy to exchange shirts with his opponent Norman Hunter. But when he attempted to join his team-mates to collect his winner's medal, Webb was stopped by an official who refused to believe he was a Chelsea footballer. Webb did eventually get his gong, in the dressing room after the ceremony.

— A VISIT FROM THE REVEREND —

Newcastle United were busy preparing for the 1908 Cup final meeting with Wolverhampton Wanderers when suddenly the changing room door opened and in walked a man of the cloth, who proceeded to say a prayer for a Wolves victory. His name was the Reverend Kenneth Hunt, and he was a Wolves player as well as an ordained minister. His prayers worked, apparently, as unfancied Wolves not only won 3–1, but Hunt scored the first goal.

— HOT-SHOT GREAVES ON THE BALL —

In 1962, Spurs' magnificent striker Jimmy Greaves was at the top of his game, scoring goals by the shedload and seemingly at will. Prior to their FA Cup final against Burnley, Greaves cheekily predicted that he would score in four minutes. In the event, he was wrong. He scored after three minutes and Spurs went on to win the match 3–1.

— THE GREATEST FINAL FIVE MINUTES? —

There have been many memorable FA Cup finals, but few events to compare with the climax of the duel in the sun between Arsenal and Manchester United in 1979.

With fewer than five minutes left, the Gunners led 2–0 through Brian Talbot and Frank Stapleton. Then, in just 115 seconds, the game was turned around. First defender Gordon McQueen stabbed the ball home from close range; then, soon after the restart, Sammy McIlroy's shot was deflected past Pat Jennings for the shock equaliser.

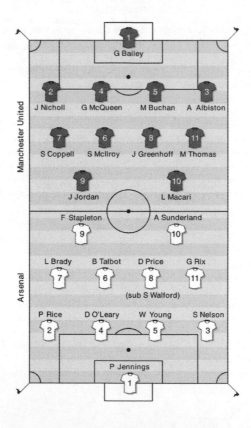

It seemed that extra time was a certainty, yet there was still a chance for one more Arsenal attack. Socks round his ankles, Arsenal's Liam Brady ran at United's defence and released Graham Rix on the left. Rix's tantalising cross was met at the back post by Alan Sunderland, who stretched out a leg to divert it into the net past Gary Bailey.

There was barely time for another restart. Referee Challis's whistle went for the end of the game and Arsenal had won an unforgettable contest.

— A NET INVENTION —

They might seem the product of a fairly straightforward idea, but someone had to invent them. The man who did invent goal-nets, used for the first time in the 1892 Cup final, was one John Alexander Brodie. Later he became chief engineer of the Mersey Tunnel.

— PENALTY CLAUSE —

After a 1–1 draw, then a 0–0 draw in the replay after extra time, Liverpool and Portsmouth brought their marathon 1992 FA Cup semi-final to a conclusion by means of a penalty shoot-out, which Liverpool duly won. Although the games themselves were forgettable, the tie was the first semi-final to be decided on penalties.

— CELTS KNOCKED OUT —

Although they provided a number of teams who contested the English FA Cup in the early years, the Scottish and Irish Football Associations were also running their own knockout competitions. In 1888, concerned that their own tournaments were being diluted, they made the unilateral decision to ban their member teams from entering the FA Cup. The Welsh FA decided to stick it out – and were rewarded in 1927 when Cardiff City beat Arsenal in the Wembley final.

— DREAMS COME TRUE —

The night before the 1913 Cup final, Aston Villa's Clem Stephenson dreamt that his team beat Sunderland with a headed goal. The next day, with just 15 minutes to go, Villa's Tommy Barber got his head to a cross and the ball flew into the net for the only goal of the game.

— GIANT-KILLING PEDIGREE —

Wimbledon stunned the footballing world in 1988 when they beat Liverpool 1–0 in the FA Cup final. But their giant-killing Cup pedigree had already been long established. In 1975, as a Southern League team, the Dons took the scalp of First Division giants Burnley in the third round. Despite this, it was another three years before they were admitted into the Fourth Division.

— HOLDING HANDS WITH CLOUGHIE —

As a mark of respect and solidarity, and to prove that the 1991 FA Cup final between Nottingham Forest and Tottenham would be played in a friendly atmosphere, respective managers Brian Clough and Terry Venables held hands as they led their teams out on to the Wembley pitch. Within 15 minutes, Paul Gascoigne had been sent off for apparently trying to kick Gary Charles into the royal box.

— BRASSED OFF —

Fifty pounds was a lot of money in 1939, and after beating Wolves in the Cup final, Portsmouth's victorious players were delighted to receive it in the form of a collective bonus from their grateful bosses. That was until they discovered that the brass band which had been entertaining the crowd at half-time had been paid £60 for their ten minutes on the pitch.

— ALL OURS —

'The FA Cup final is the greatest single match outside the World Cup final – and it's ours.'
– Sir Bobby Robson.

— COVENTRY TAKE THE HONOURS —

Tottenham were overwhelming favourites to win the 1987 FA Cup final, not only because of their regal progress to Wembley that year but because in seven previous visits they had never lost a match. In contrast their opponents, Coventry City, managed by the oddball duo of John Sillett and George Curtis, were Cup interlopers, reaching their first final in 104 years of trying.

When Clive Allen put the Londoners ahead after two minutes, even the most optimistic Cup romantics resigned themselves to a one-sided affair. The Cup, though, was about to throw up yet another of its stirring dramas.

Gary Bennett, a loser as a Manchester City player in the 1981 final against Tottenham, equalised after nine minutes, but Tottenham's inspirational skipper Gary Mabbutt put the Londoners back in front five minutes before the interval.

Again Coventry came back, this time veteran striker Keith Houchen – a penalty hero with York City against Arsenal two years previously – flinging himself at a Dave Bennett cross and heading sensationally past Ray Clemence in the Tottenham goal. A breathless Wembley steeled itself for extra time, but there was one more cruel throw of the dice to come.

Perhaps fearing that another half-hour would be a step too far, Coventry pressed hard and were rewarded in the dying minutes when a Lloyd McGrath cross bounced off Mabbutt's knee before spiralling over the despairing hands of Clemence.

It was hard on Mabbutt and on a Tottenham side who had played with flair and appetite, and who had contributed manfully to one of the great FA Cup finals.

— FINALISTS FLOP —

Having both reached the Cup final against the odds the previous year, West Ham and Fulham were duly bombed out of the 1976 competition in the third round. It was the first time it had happened since 1932, when neither West Bromwich Albion nor Everton made it past the first hurdle after appearing at Wembley.

— THIRD-PLACE PLAY-OFF —

Between 1970 and 1974, third-place matches were held between the beaten Cup semi-finalists. Much like the third-place play-offs in the World Cup, the matches were uniformly rubbish, with neither side in the slightest bit interested in prolonging the agony of failing to reach the final. The misguided innovation was scrapped in 1975 to universal approval.

— VALIANT NO-HOPERS —

Non-League Marlow are the only team to have played in every FA Cup tournament, although success has proved elusive. As Great Marlow they were beaten semi-finalists in 1881–82, but since the start of the 20th century their best run was to make it to the third round in 1992–93, when they were hammered 5–1 by Tottenham Hotspur.

— TIE A WHITE RIBBON . . . —

After their historic win in 1901, non-League Tottenham Hotspur created one of the Cup's most cherished traditions when they became the first to tie ribbons in their team colours around the handles of the trophy.

— CUP FINAL DAY —

The first 11 FA Cup finals were played in March, before being switched to April in 1885. In 1937 the big day was switched to May, before reverting to April the following year, where it stayed until 1952. Finally it was then switched back to May where it has remained ever since.

— WEATHER WIPEOUT —

In 1979 the entire FA Cup fourth round was wiped out by the weather for the first time in the history of the competition. The only First Division game played that day was between Everton and Southampton on a pitch which Toffees boss Gordon Lee described scathingly as a 'death-trap'.

— GET BACK TO WORK —

The FA have always prided themselves on being above government interference – but in 1946, when 80,000 people turned up to watch a semi-final replay between Derby County and Birmingham City on a Wednesday afternoon when they should have been at work, Downing Street was furious. Soon afterwards, midweek afternoon matches were stopped.

— JUST IN CASE —

After Liverpool's over-exuberant stars dented the newly remade FA Cup in 1992, the FA took the understandable decision to have a replica made – just in case. The second trophy is locked away in a bank vault, presumably in case Liverpool win it again!

— WHITE HORSE BRIDGE —

After a lot of deliberation and a public vote, in May 2005 a new footbridge at Wembley Stadium was named the White Horse Bridge in honour of the heroics of police horse Billy and his rider PC George Scorey at the 1923 Cup final.

— FOREST FINALLY BEATEN —

Frank Stapleton's goal for Arsenal in the second half of their fifth-round tie against Nottingham Forest in February 1979 not only put Brian Clough's side out of the Cup that year, it signalled Forest's first defeat at the City Ground since April 1977.

— GROUND RULES —

In 1909 both Nottingham Forest and Notts County were given home ties in the first round. Resigned to the fact that most Nottingham football fans supported Forest, County sold home advantage to their opponents, Bradford City, for the princely sum of £1,000. It proved to be a lousy deal for both clubs: County lost 4–2, and Bradford failed to recoup the £1,000 in gate money.

— THE MORTENSEN FINAL? —

'Poor Stan Mortensen. People forget it was him that scored a hat-trick. It really should be called the Stan Mortensen final, you know.'
– Sir Stanley Matthews on the 1953 'Matthews Final'.

— NICE TO SEE YOU AGAIN —

When West Bromwich Albion played Leeds United in a fifth-round replay in 1979, it was the seventh time the two sides had met each other in all competitions that season. On this occasion, the Baggies ran out 2–0 winners.

— THE FA SHED NO LIGHT —

Floodlit games were not officially sanctioned by the FA until the 1950s, largely due to a disastrous experiment carried out by Celtic a couple of years earlier. They had the bright idea of hanging lights from wires suspended above the pitch – which worked fine until a couple of up-and-unders brought the whole edifice crashing down on to the playing surface.

— EARLY CROWD CONTROL —

In 1913 a massive crowd of 120,081 fans packed into Crystal Palace to watch the FA Cup final between Sunderland and Aston Villa. In the absence of fencing and stewards, the organisers had to rely on a rope and British good manners to keep the crowd from straying on to the pitch. Needless to say it worked.

— CURRIE GIVES HODDLE THE RUNS —

This was the famous slogan on a banner displayed by Queen's Park Rangers fans, celebrating the fact that their star player Tony Currie was about to go up against Tottenham wizard Glenn Hoddle in the 1982 Cup final. In the event, it was the other way round. After a 1–1 draw, Spurs won the replay 1–0 – the goal scored from the penalty spot by Hoddle after a foul by Currie.

— THE WHITE HORSE FINAL —

With a capacity of 127,000, the FA were so confident that the new Wembley Stadium would have room for everyone who wanted to see the 1923 Cup final between West Ham and Bolton that they didn't even bother issuing tickets.

It was a miscalculation which would cause total chaos, and ensure that this particular occasion would be immortalised in FA Cup legend.

The date was 28 April, and on a bright, sunny morning the crowds started arriving early. By one o'clock the terraces were full and, when the gates closed 45 minutes later, the stadium was bursting at the seams with more than 200,000 spectators and a further 50,000 clamouring outside.

As kick-off approached, the tide could no longer be held back. The gates were rushed and tens of thousands of fans flooded into the ground. For those already inside there was nowhere to go but on to the pitch itself, and within minutes the playing surface was under a sea of people.

That no-one was injured in the melee was a testament to those admirable British qualities of even temper and good humour, as was the fact that the game was able to kick off just 45 minutes late.

Stars of the show were a 13-year-old white police horse called Billy and his rider, Constable George Scorey, who expertly manoeuvred the crowds to the touchlines and managed to keep them there in good order for the duration of the game.

With the ball and the players regularly disappearing into the crowd, the match eventually ended 2–0 to Bolton, with the Trotters' David Jack becoming the first player to score at Wembley Stadium.

All that was forgotten, however, as the heroics of Billy and Constable Scorey meant that Wembley's inaugural game would go down in history as the 'White Horse Final'.

— GAZZA'S KNEE —

In the Wembley semi-final against Arsenal, Tottenham's Paul Gascoigne had rifled home a stunning 30-yard free-kick to take the White Hart Lane side into the 1991 final to face Nottingham Forest.

But some 15 minutes into the match, the larger-than-life Geordie was to make an even bigger impact at the same end of the pitch when he recklessly tackled Forest defender Gary Charles and ruptured the anterior cruciate ligament of his right knee.

Stretchered off the pitch in tears, Gazza watched the rest of the match from a hospital bed as Spurs went on to win 2–1, thanks to an injury-time own-goal by Des Walker.

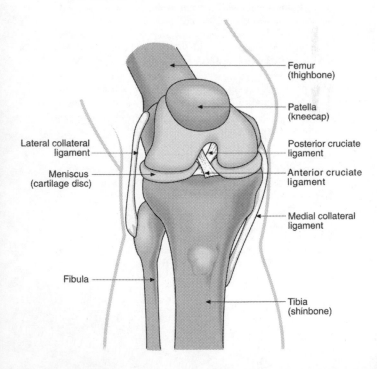

— SNEAK THIEF SCORES A WINNER —

Cardiff City were delighted when they met Queen's Park Rangers in the third round in 1990 because the match produced record receipts. But before the Welsh club could decide how to spend the money, it had gone. A thief read about the takings in the local newspaper, broke into the ground and stole it before it could be banked.

— BAILEY'S MUTI MAGIC —

Having conceded seven goals in his three previous Wembley finals, Manchester United's South African-born keeper Gary Bailey decided a little home cure was required for the 1983 replay against Brighton. This came in the form of a tribal 'muti', a superstitious ritual which involved tying coloured ribbons to the goalposts and fixing a padlock to the goal-net. It worked like a charm: United cruised to a 4–0 victory.

— THE HAVES AND THE HAVE-NOTS —

When First Division high-flyers Arsenal played Third Division Walsall in the third round in 1932–33, Highbury manager Herbert Chapman raided his club's coffers and splashed out £87 to kit the team out with new boots. This was more than the whole of the Walsall team cost to assemble – and the scheme backfired spectacularly when the underdogs stunned the nation by winning 2–0.

— ARGY BARGY —

If anyone needs proof that modern goalkeepers are a protected species, look no further than the 1958 Cup final between Manchester United and Bolton Wanderers. Already leading 1–0, Bolton secured the win when United 'keeper Harry Gregg caught a ball on his own goal line and was promptly shoulder-charged into the back of the net by Bolton's combative hit-man Nat Lofthouse. There were no complaints, because back then shoulder-charging was an accepted part of the game.

— THE MYSTERY OF THE DRAW —

'When I arrived in the basement press room at the Football Association's offices in Russell Square, a little platoon of scribblers was already assembled, with sharpened pencils in front of them, and thin sheets of paper with pieces of carbon in between. They are exasperating people, though, these officers of the Football Association. They assemble immediately after lunch, yet do all sorts of footling things before they come to the real business of the day.

'At length, however, there comes a hint that the draw is actually being made, so we make sure that our pencils are really sharp. Funnily enough, on the day the draw for the second round was made the electric light in that basement room failed about five minutes before the important news came along. Fortunately, by drawing the blind a little higher, we could just see to write. Outside, peering into the press room, were a score or more of London boys and girls. Probably not one of them had ever seen a Cup tie, but they knew that the draw for the second round was being made.

'At last the returning officer arrived with his sheet of paper. In he came, and locked the door, mysteriously, silently. "Are you ready, gentlemen?" he asked. We were. And then the door was unlocked, and hot-footed messenger boys dashed off with the news to the offices of the London newspapers and the news agencies. But I have never seen the draw made – no man has who is not an officer of the Football Association. The Council Chamber, in which the draw is made, is bolted and barred against all unofficial comers.'
– J Harwood Lee, *The Penny Pictorial* (1921).

— BOURNEMOUTH GET THE HUMP —

Having been elected that year into the Football League, Bournemouth were most put out in 1923 when the FA refused to put them straight into the first round and instead paired them with unheard-of Portsea Gas Company in the qualifiers. In fact, the Cherries were so disgusted they withdrew from the competition entirely.

— LUCKY DARLO —

In 1999 Darlington claimed an unusual place in FA Cup history when they played in the third round – having already been knocked out in the second. The reason for their reinstatement was that they were the so-called lucky losers, drawn by the FA to replace Manchester United, who that year decided to play in the World Club Championship in Brazil instead.

— A MAN OF HIS WORD —

Clearly not expecting to win, Colchester manager Dick Graham announced that if his side beat Leeds United in the Cup in 1971 he would scale the walls of Colchester Castle. The minnows won 3–2 and the next day Graham scaled the walls – all 30ft to the very top.

— WINNING BROTHERS —

In 1904 there were big celebrations in the Maley household and two trophies on the family mantelpiece. Tom was manager of Manchester City, who beat Bolton 1–0 in the FA Cup final, while brother Willie was in charge of the Celtic team who lifted the Scottish Cup after defeating Rangers 3–2 at Hampden Park.

— BURY RECORD BREAKERS —

Bury's 6–0 demolition of Derby County in 1903 remains a record margin of victory in an FA Cup final. It was most definitely the Shakers' year. In the Cup run they did not concede a goal – becoming only the second side to achieve the feat, after Preston North End managed it four years earlier.

— THE POWER OF 1 —

It was said of Tottenham Hotspur that as long as the year ended with a '1' they would win the FA Cup. The facts prove it – sort of. After lifting the trophy in 1901 they went on to win it in 1921, 1961, 1981 and 1991. Mind you, they also won it in 1962, 1967 and 1982.

— LUCKY JOE —

Joe Smith, manager of Blackpool's 1953 Cup-winning team, was no stranger to Wembley glory. He'd previously earned winner's medals as a player in 1923 and 1926 – with Blackpool's 1953 opponents Bolton Wanderers.

— THE DUSTBIN FINAL —

Wolves won the 1960 FA Cup final with a combination of crunching tackles and soft refereeing. At least, that was the verdict of many Blackburn Rovers fans, who pelted the players with apple-cores and orange-peel as they came off the pitch. As a result, the game is forever known as 'The Dustbin Final'.

— ACTION REPLAY —

In the early years of the FA Cup, replays were seen as the only fair way of deciding a result in the wake of a drawn game. But after the finals of 1910, 1911 and 1912 all went to replays, the FA decided that enough was enough and extra time was brought in for the Cup final of 1913. It was not required, as Aston Villa beat Sunderland 1–0.

— WORTH THE WAIT FOR WREXHAM —

The cold winter of 1979 resulted in dozens of games being wiped out. In the FA Cup, the third-round tie between Wrexham and Stockport County was postponed an amazing nine times before finally being given the go-ahead in February. Wrexham wasted no time once the game kicked off, romping to a 6–2 victory.

— SCOTTISH SHORTLIST —

Manchester United boss Sir Alex Ferguson is one of only two men to manage Scottish and English Cup-winning teams. Jimmy Cochrane (Kilmarnock 1929, Sunderland 1937) was the first. Ferguson led Aberdeen to Scottish Cup successes in 1983, 1984 and 1986.

— THE GOAL THAT NEVER WAS —

Under visionary manager Herbert Chapman, Arsenal had swept all before them in the League and were, in 1932, close to becoming the game's most dominant force. In that year's final against Newcastle United, an early goal suggested that winning the Cup would be a mere formality.

The result would hinge, however, on Newcastle's 38th-minute equaliser, a goal which even today has Gooners spitting feathers at the injustice of it all.

It seemed a lost cause as United's Jimmy Richardson chased a long pass towards the Arsenal byline, but somehow he managed to hook it back across the box with his right foot. Jack Allen was on hand to slot the ball home from six yards.

To all present, it had seemed obvious that the ball had been well over the byline before the cross – but for some reason, probably because he and his linesmen were 30 yards behind the play, referee W P Harper allowed the goal to stand.

Although they bit their collective tongue, Arsenal were clearly rattled and when Allen struck again on 72 minutes the Cup was heading for Tyneside.

The incident made front-page headlines the next day, relegating a story about the success of Adolf Hitler's Nazi party in the German elections to the inside pages.

Arsenal were to suffer yet more indignity the following year when they were turfed out of the Cup in the third round by lowly Walsall of the Third Division (North).

— SUBSTITUTES BETWEEN THE STICKS —

Paul Jones of Southampton became the first goalkeeper to come on as a substitute in the FA Cup final when he replaced the injured Antii Niemi against Arsenal in 2003. The following year, Manchester United's Roy Carroll replaced Tim Howard in their FA Cup final against Millwall.

— GATE RECEIPTS —

The gross gate receipts for the notorious White Horse Final of 1923, when more than 200,000 spectators crammed into the new Wembley Stadium, were officially £27,776, of which £4,026 was paid out in entertainment tax, £4,714 to the British Empire Exhibition, £6,365 each to the two clubs, and the same amount to the FA. The FA also refunded £2,797 to ticket holders who were unable to find their seats in the melee.

— WATKIN'S FOLLY —

Had it been left to noted architect Sir Edward Watkin, Wembley Stadium might never have been built. In 1923 Watkin wanted to build a huge tower on the site, to rival the Eiffel Tower in Paris. Fortunately for football, the project never got further than the foundations, which shifted shortly after being laid.

— WAINWRIGHT'S GUIDE TO THE CUP FINAL —

He might have been famed for his *Pictorial Guides to the Lake District*, but Alfred Wainwright was also a fanatical Blackburn Rovers fan. Such was his enthusiasm for the club that in 1940, as one of the founders of the supporters' club, he organised a coach trip to take fans on the long journey south to watch the team in action in the wartime final against West Ham.

— SWEET SEVEN FOR KEANO —

When he turned out for Manchester United in the 2005 final against Arsenal, Roy Keane set a modern record by appearing in his seventh FA Cup final, with only Lord Kinnaird playing in more. Keane played in the 1991 final with Nottingham Forest and the finals of 1994, 1995, 1996, 1999 and 2004 with United. Lord Kinnaird played in nine of the first 11 finals in the 1870s and 1880s.

— NEW BALLS, PLEASE —

The 1973 match between Leeds United and Sunderland was the last time an orange ball was used in an FA Cup final.

— UNIQUELY BUCHAN —

Martin Buchan is the only player to have captained a team which won the Scottish Cup – that was Aberdeen in 1970 – as well as one which won the English FA Cup, Manchester United in 1977.

— LATE SHOW FOR LINIGHAN —

Arsenal's Andy Linighan scored the latest FA Cup final goal in open play when he headed the winner – despite a broken nose – in the last minute of extra time in the replayed 1993 final against Sheffield Wednesday. That put Arsenal 2–1 up and the referee blew for time 44 seconds later.

— A GONG FOR THE YANK —

In 2004 Manchester United goalkeeper Tim Howard became the first American to earn an FA Cup winner's medal, following his appearance in the 3–0 victory over Millwall at Cardiff's Millennium Stadium.

— THE AMATEUR SPIRIT —

Preston North End fielded amateur goalkeepers in their first two appearances in the FA Cup final. Dr Mills Roberts was the custodian in 1889, then James Frederick Mitchell guarded the net in 1922.

— I'LL BE YOUR SUBSTITUTE —

West Bromwich Albion's Dennis Clarke was the first substitute to be used in an FA Cup final when he replaced John Kaye against Everton in 1968. Albion won 1–0 with a Jeff Astle goal in extra time.

— A QUESTION OF PRIORITIES —

The kick-off of the 1873 final between Wanderers and Oxford University was brought forward to 11am to allow players and their friends to watch the Boat Race, which was rowed on the same day.

— MOTTY'S FA CUP MOMENTS —

The FA Cup has given me so many great memories as a commentator and a fan over the years that it's almost impossible to narrow them down. But if I was to choose my ten favourite moments, I suppose they would have to include the following:

1. **The 1950 Cup final, Arsenal v Liverpool.** This was the first Cup final I saw as a kid. My father was a mad keen football fan and he took me to a music shop in South London called Drysdales, where we watched the match on a black-and-white TV with a nine-inch screen. Three years later we watched the Matthews final at the house of some family friends called the Peppers, who lived in Deptford. It's funny what you remember!

2. **The 1964 Cup final, West Ham United v Preston North End.** This was the first Cup final I ever saw live at Wembley. I went with my dad and he'd managed to get seats right next to the steps leading up to the royal box. It was a fantastic match which West Ham won 3–2, but the highlight of the day for me was being able to lean across and touch the great Bobby Moore as he went up to collect the trophy. Two years later, of course, he climbed the same steps to receive the World Cup.

3. **The 1970 Cup final, Chelsea v Leeds.** I had just joined the BBC as a young radio reporter, and I was thrilled – not to mention terrified – to be assigned the job of roving reporter in the build-up to the Cup final. One of the most daunting prospects was interviewing Leeds United's manager Don Revie, who, like his team, had a no-nonsense reputation and did not suffer fools gladly. In those days we had to record the interview, then run the tape to the small BBC studio at the other end of the stadium, where it was edited. You can imagine how I felt when, having successfully interviewed Revie, I raced to the studio to discover that the tape hadn't recorded properly! Fortunately, Revie was happy to do it again.

4. **The 1977 Cup final, Manchester United v Liverpool.** My debut as an FA Cup final commentator, and one of the proudest days of my life. There was I, following in the illustrious footsteps of giants like Kenneth Wolstenholme and David Coleman. The game was decided in a thrilling five-minute spell just after half-time when, having had a goal by Stuart Pearson cancelled out by Liverpool's Jimmy Case, Manchester United went up the other end of the pitch and scored again through a combination of Lou Macari and Jimmy Greenhoff.

5. **Hereford United v Newcastle United.** The date 5 February 1972 is one that will always be special to me. It was fourth-round day, but as one of the BBC's most junior commentators I was despatched to muddy Edgar Street to cover the much-postponed third-round tie between First Division Newcastle United and non-League Hereford. Although Hereford had surprised everyone by holding the Magpies to a 2–2 draw at St James's Park, nobody expected a repeat performance – let alone one of the great FA Cup shocks of all time. Ronnie Radford's 35-yard thunderbolt, and my excited shout of 'What a goal!', is still broadcast every year on third-round day. They say everyone needs a break: well, that goal and that match certainly put me on the map as a commentator.

6. **Sutton United v Coventry City, 1989.** The FA Cup has a habit of unearthing great characters, and one of my favourites was Barrie Williams, the jovial, Shakespeare-quoting manager of non-League Sutton United. Barrie had been in charge of the Gander Green Lane club for a decade, but we all came to know and love him in the weeks leading up to Sutton's third-round tie at home to Coventry City. In those days, Coventry were in the top five of Division One, and had won the Cup just two years earlier. But in one of the great upsets, Sutton deservedly beat them 2–1 with goals by Tony Rains and Matty Hanlan. Magic stuff! Barrie normally had a quote for every occasion, but on that day I think it was the first time he was lost for words.

7. **The 1981 Cup final, Tottenham Hotspur v Manchester City.** Ask almost anyone which modern Cup Final stands out in their memory, and the chances are they'll say this one. The 100th Wembley final had everything – excitement, passion, joy and heartbreak. It also featured one of the great FA Cup goals of all time, scored by the Argentine Ricky Villa in the replay. It's often forgotten that in the first game, which was drawn 1–1, Villa had a stinker and was substituted. I'll never forget watching him trudging disconsolately around the pitch to the dressing room. Who would have known that just five days later he would be the hero of the hour? Tottenham also featured in one of my favourite Wembley finals, in 1987 against Coventry City. Twice a goal down, Coventry not only equalised twice but went on to win the game thanks to Gary Mabbutt's own-goal. Mind you, Keith Houchen's diving header was worthy of winning any final.

— MOTTY'S FA CUP MOMENTS (CONT'D) —

8. **The 1986 Cup final, Liverpool v Everton; the 1994 Cup final, Manchester United v Chelsea.** Completing the League and FA Cup double is always a special achievement, and on two occasions I've been present when great clubs have done it for the first time. The first was in 1986 when Liverpool beat Everton 3–1 to win the first all-Merseyside derby at Wembley. The second was in 1994 when an Eric Cantona-inspired Manchester United thrashed Chelsea 4–0. Both results were very much a vindication of the respective managers. There had been raised eyebrows on the Kop when the inspirational Kenny Dalglish was installed as player-manager that season, but his star-studded side were deserved double winners. Later, it had been just four years since Alex Ferguson had been on the verge of getting the sack from Old Trafford. In that time he had built a side which would dominate British football for a decade.

9. **The 1979 Cup final, Arsenal v Manchester United.** This was actually a pretty humdrum game until the last five minutes. But what a last five minutes they were! Having dominated the match, Arsenal suddenly found their two-goal lead cancelled out, only to go up to the other end of the pitch and score the most dramatic of winners through Alan Sunderland. The goal was set up initially by Liam Brady, who was magnificent that day. Another late show which sticks in the memory was in 2001, when two goals in the last eight minutes by Michael Owen snatched victory for Liverpool against Arsenal.

10. **Liverpool v Rochdale, 1996.** The FA Cup has had its share of heroes – Dave Beasant, Stanley Matthews, Bert Trautmann, Ricky Villa, Roberto Di Matteo – but for me the greatest of all has to be Ian Rush of Liverpool. His goal in this 7–0 third-round rout brought his Cup tally to an astonishing 42, including five in three finals – a record which he later stretched to 43 and which will take some beating. He also picked up three winner's medals in 1986, 1989 and 1992. The only player to get near Rushie in my book is Bryan Robson, another FA Cup great, who lifted the trophy on three occasions as skipper of Manchester United.

— BROLLY GOOD SHOW, PRESTON —

When Preston North End beat Reading 18–0 in a rainstorm during an FA Cup tie in 1894, the Preston goalkeeper watched much of the game from under an umbrella.

— LIGHT AND SHADE —

Although the 1968 FA Cup final between West Bromwich Albion and Everton was shown in glorious colour on TV, the European Cup final, staged at Wembley a few days later between Manchester United and Benfica, was in grainy black-and-white. Why? Because the European game was played under flood-lights, and the BBC's colour cameras couldn't work in the twilight.

— THE LAWMAN BEATEN BY NATURE —

In a fourth-round FA Cup clash with Luton in 1961, Denis Law scored all six goals for Manchester City as they stormed into a 6–2 lead. Sadly for the Scot, 'storm' became the operative word as the match was abandoned because of torrential rain and his goals were struck from the record books. He did manage another one in the replayed match, but to no avail: City lost 3–1 and were out of the Cup.

— FOREIGN FIELDS —

The 2001 final between Arsenal and Liverpool was the first in the 129-year history of the competition in which both teams were managed by foreigners. Frenchman Arsene Wenger was bidding to win the trophy for the second time with Arsenal, but it was his compatriot, Gerard Houllier, who secured Liverpool's first Cup success since 1992.

— MASTER BLASTER —

In 1880 Henry Cursham of Notts County scored two goals in his first FA Cup tie against hapless Derbyshire FC. He clearly liked the competition and, by the time he retired seven years later, he had blasted no fewer than 48 FA Cup goals – a record which still stands. His impressive tally included seven hat-tricks, and there is still dispute whether he scored six or nine in an 11–1 thrashing of Wednesbury Strollers in 1881.

— FANTASTIC FERGIE —

Manchester United's Alex Ferguson is the most successful manager in FA Cup history with five wins, in 1990, 1994, 1996, 1999 and 2004. His only defeats in the final were against Everton in 1995 and Arsenal in 2005. In taking Manchester United to a seventh final in 2005 he beat the record of Frank Watt, who led Newcastle United to six finals between 1905 and 1924.

— TRUE BLUE (AND RED) SCOUSER —

Gary Ablett is the only Merseyside-born player to win the FA Cup with both Liverpool (1989 versus Everton) and Everton (1995 versus Manchester United).

— STEVE'S CUP BLOOMER —

In a career which lasted from 1892 to 1914, the great Steve Bloomer scored 352 League goals and played 23 times for England – making him a true soccer legend. Yet despite featuring in two finals for Derby County, the one medal which eluded Bloomer was that of an FA Cup winner.

— HOWAY HAMANN! —

When Dietmar Hamann appeared for Newcastle United in the 1999 final against Manchester United, he was the first German national to play in the domestic game's gala fixture since Bert Trautmann, Manchester City's goalkeeping hero of 1956. In 2005 Arsenal's Jens Lehmann became the first German custodian since Trautmann to appear in the final.

— HOT-SHOT TOPHAM —

Unquestioned star of the 1893 Cup-winning Wolverhampton Wanderers side was right-winger Dick Topham. Not only was he a brilliant dribbler, but also he possessed a thunderbolt of a shot. During the final one long-range effort hit a watching policeman with such venom that it knocked him clean off his feet and into the crowd.

— UNBEATABLE PYM —

Bolton Wanderers goalkeeper Dick Pym collected three FA Cup winner's medals, in 1923, 1926 and 1929, and never conceded a goal at Wembley. He also lived longer than any other England international.

— NINE TO MACDOUGALL —

The most individual goals in an FA Cup tie came on 20 November 1971, when Ted MacDougall of Bournemouth scored an astonishing NINE times against Margate in the first round.

— BETTER LATE THAN NEVER —

The first FA Cup winners, Wanderers, didn't receive the trophy directly after the final whistle. Instead they had to wait nearly a month until their annual dinner at the Pall Mall restaurant in London, when it was presented to the victorious skipper by FA president Ebenezer Cobb Morley.

— THE FA CUP 1, THE LUFTWAFFE 0 —

In January 1941 the FA Cup was being stored for the duration of the war in a Portsmouth bank vault. For some reason it was decided to move it to the safe-keeping of another bank in a different part of town. That night, a German bombing raid flattened the original bank.

— IS IT A BIRD? —

Seven years after the White Horse Final, another Wembley showpiece would become overshadowed by events that had nothing to do with the game. As Huddersfield and Arsenal battled it out on the pitch, a silver German Graf Zeppelin appeared in the sky above them. As the crowd booed and jeered, the mighty airship dipped its nose respectfully to King George V and moved slowly on.

— MEMORABILIA —

Arsenal's club museum opened in 1993. Among its many exhibits are the shirt worn by Alex James in the 1936 final, the boot with which Charlie George hit the winner against Liverpool in 1971, and the red open-topped bus in which Arsenal's winning teams have paraded around North London.

— THE FASTEST GOAL —

Having already watched their side lose the League Cup and suffer relegation from the Premiership in the space of just a few days, Middlesbrough fans nevertheless hoped that imported stars like Juninho, Emerson and Ravanelli would lift the gloom in the 1997 FA Cup final against Chelsea. After a mere 42 seconds, that notion appeared fanciful. That was how long it took the Londoners to take the lead through Italian midfielder Roberto Di Matteo, with a spectacular strike which became the fastest goal ever scored in a Wembley Cup final.

 25 secs Middlesbrough's Robbie Mustoe is tackled by Dennis Wise inside Chelsea half

Wise passes to Di Matteo inside his own half **32 secs**

 36 secs Di Matteo runs into the Middlesbrough half unchallenged

Up ahead Chelsea's Mark Hughes makes a crossfield run which drags away Middlesbrough defender Nigel Pearson, leaving Di Matteo a clear view on goal **38 secs**

 40 secs Di Matteo fires in the shot from 25 yards out

— THE FA CUP FIRST TEAM —

- **Dave Beasant** (Wimbledon), the first goalkeeper to save a penalty in a Cup final.
- **Roberto Di Matteo** (Chelsea), scorer of Wembley's fastest goal after 42 seconds.
- **Curtis Weston** (Millwall), at 17 years 119 days the youngest finalist in the history of the Cup.
- **Brian Greenhoff** (Manchester United), one of the first brothers to play on the winning side in a Cup final, the other being:
- **Jimmy Greenhoff** (Manchester United).
- **David Jack** (Bolton Wanderers), scorer of Wembley's first goal in 1923.
- **Kevin Moran** (Manchester United), first player to be dismissed in a Cup final.
- **Ian Callaghan** (Liverpool), played in a record 88 FA Cup matches.
- **Ian Rush** (Liverpool), scored a record five Cup final goals: two in 1986, two in 1989 and one in 1992.
- **Morton Peto Betts** (Wanderers), scorer of the first FA Cup final goal in 1872.
- **John Aldridge** (Liverpool), first man to miss a penalty at Wembley.
- **Dennis Clarke** (West Bromwich Albion), the first substitute to be used in a Cup final in 1968.

— THE GREAT FA CUP MYSTERY —

Delighted with their 1–0 win over West Midlands rivals West Bromwich Albion in the 1895 Cup final, Aston Villa decided to show off their silverware in the shop window of a local cobbler, William Shillcock.

Five months later, it was stolen – and, despite a national outcry, the 'little tin idol' was never seen again.

The mystery of who pinched the trophy (the only clue was a size-five footprint in the shop window) and what happened to it, remains to this day, although there has been no shortage of suspects in the intervening century.

In 1958, *The Sunday Pictorial* carried a front-page confession by an 82-year-old jailbird named Harry Burge. But upon closer examination, Burge's story was found to be riddled with discrepancies and he was quickly discredited.

In 1975 the finger was pointed at Joseph Piercewright, a renowned coin-counterfeiter who, it was claimed, had melted down the trophy shortly after stealing it. Again the story failed to hold water and the mystery remained.

But most intriguing of all was the testimony in 1996 of 80-year-old Gladys Stait of Birmingham, who revealed that her husband Jack had once admitted that his dad had 'pinched the Cup out of Shillcock's window' and melted it down for ten shillings.

The culprit's name was John Stait, known as 'Stosher' because of his luxurious moustache. To this day, he remains the likeliest candidate – although the true identity of the thief will probably never be known.

— LILLIE BRIDGE —

One of the perks of being the first winners of the FA Cup was the right to choose the venue for the next final. In 1873, Wanderers selected Lillie Bridge in West Brompton, as it was conveniently situated for most of its well-heeled players. It was the only time the final was ever played there.

— A CUP FOR ALL —

When Wanderers won the Cup for the third time in a row in 1878, it meant they were entitled to keep the trophy in perpetuity. However, they gave it back to the Football Association on condition that no team in the future could ever win it outright.

— THE ROCHDALE WHIPPET —

Yorkshireman Alan Taylor was the undisputed star of West Ham's 1975 Cup run. As well as the two goals which sunk Fulham in the final, the man known as 'The Rochdale Whippet' also bagged two in the quarter-final against Arsenal and a brace against Ipswich Town in the semi. It was a remarkable record considering Taylor had started the season playing Fourth Division football with Rochdale.

— THE CURSE OF DERBY —

Derby County put their long-standing failure to win the Cup down to a gypsy curse which had been placed on their ground. In 1946 skipper Jack Nicholas was persuaded to visit a local gypsy camp during the week before the final. The curse was lifted in return for silver, and Derby went on to win the Cup for the first time, emphatically beating Charlton 4–1.

— THE END OF CHANGING —

The 1875 final between Royal Engineers and Old Etonians was the first time teams were not obliged to change ends after every goal. It was also the first time wooden crossbars were used instead of tape.

— WHO WOULD HAVE BET? —

Interviewed prior to the 1946 final, referee E D Smith of Sunderland solemnly declared that the chances of the ball bursting during the match were a million to one. Not only did the ball explode during the game, but it also burst again the following year when Charlton beat Burnley 1–0.

— BERT TRAUTMANN'S NECK —

Footballers have it easy these days. When Bert Trautmann turned out for Manchester City in the 1956 final against Birmingham, the 33-year-old German-born goalkeeper had already fought as a paratrooper on the Russian front, been captured, escaped, and been captured again by the British, and interned in a POW camp in Manchester for the rest of the war.

When he signed for City in 1949, 40,000 people took to the streets of Manchester and demonstrated against the signing of a German soldier, holding banners daubed with slogans like 'Off with the German'.

Fortunately, Trautmann's ability between the sticks soon changed their minds and by the mid-1950s he had become a much-loved character at Maine Road. The 1956 final would cap his career in glory – but even then things did not go to plan.

In the 75th minute, with City leading 2–1, Trautmann dived courageously at the feet of Birmingham's onrushing attacker Peter Murphy and was knocked out. Despite severe pain he continued for the rest of the match, making a series of superb saves, and collected his winner's medal as City won 3–1 thanks to goals by Joe Hayes, Jack Dyson and Bobby Johnstone.

It was only three days later that an X-ray revealed that the big German had broken his neck.

It was an injury which would have ended a lesser man's career, yet Trautmann went on to appear in a total of 545 matches for City between 1949 and 1964 and won the Footballer of the Year award in 1956 for his FA Cup heroics. Amazingly, he never played for Germany, as the head coach, Sepp Herberger, refused to pick any German who plied his trade abroad.

— THE SAINTS GO CRUISING —

As a reward for beating the mighty Manchester United in the 1976 FA Cup final, the players of Second Division Southampton, together with their wives and girlfriends, were sent on an all-expenses cruise.

— HOME AND AWAY —

The decision by the FA to adopt a home-and-away format during the 1945–46 season was greeted with massive enthusiasm by fans who had been starved of football during the war years. A crowd of 80,400 – a record for a midweek game – saw Derby County wallop Birmingham 4–0 in the semi-final replay at Maine Road, Manchester.

— ABIDE WITH PAT —

Manchester United were about to take to the pitch for the 1963 final when someone noticed their Scottish wing-half Pat Crerand was missing. He was subsequently found standing in the tunnel singing 'Abide With Me', wearing nothing but a jockstrap.

— SCOTS UP FOR THE CUP —

In the 19th century seven Scottish clubs played in the English Cup. Queen's Park reached two finals and Glasgow Rangers lost to Aston Villa in a semi-final. Welsh clubs still compete to this day – and Cardiff City remain the only non-English winners of the trophy.

— PREMATURE PRESTON —

When Preston North End confidently asked to be photographed beside the Cup prior to the 1888 final, they were given short shrift by FA President Francis Marindin, who said: 'Hadn't you better win it first?' Preston duly lost 2–1 to West Bromwich Albion.

— DECADE OF THE UNDERDOG —

The 1980s heralded a remarkable streak of unfancied teams reaching Wembley finals. Queen's Park Rangers (1982), Brighton (1983), Watford (1984) and Crystal Palace (1990) all tried and failed against top-grade opposition. Coventry (1987) and Wimbledon (1988) succeeded against all the odds, defeating Tottenham and Liverpool respectively.

— NICE TO BEAT YOU, DAD —

In a first qualifying round tie in 1996, 21-year-old Nick Scaife of Bishop Auckland faced his 41-year-old dad Bobby, who was turning out for Pickering Town. Both played in midfield and Bishops, the home team, won 3–1.

— THE MERSEYSIDE FINAL —

It seems strange that it should take more than 100 years for the two Merseyside giants to meet each other in an FA Cup final, but when it finally happened in 1986 Liverpool and Everton provided a match to remember.

Trailing to Gary Lineker's strike, Liverpool surged ahead through two goals by Ian Rush and another by Australian import Craig Johnston.

The win gave Liverpool their first League and Cup double and only the third double in the 20th century, following Tottenham and Arsenal. These were two quality sides: Everton were League runners-up that year and would have won the double in 1985 had they beaten Manchester United at Wembley.

— HE'S ON – NOW HE'S OFF —

The quickest sending-off of a player in the FA Cup was at Goodison Park on 5 January 1997. The unfortunate fellow was Swindon Town defender Ian Culverhouse, who was dismissed after just 52 seconds for handling the ball on the goal line from a shot by Everton's Andrei Kanchelskis.

— SAINTS' OLD TIMERS —

People were amazed when Division Two Southampton beat Manchester United in 1976, but the Saints weren't without FA Cup final experience. Jim McCalliog had played for Sheffield Wednesday in 1966, Peter Rodrigues for Leicester in 1969, and Peter Osgood for Chelsea in 1970.

— THE YOUNGEST PLAYER . . . SO FAR —

Curtis Weston, at 17 years 119 days, is the youngest finalist in the history of the FA Cup. He played for Millwall against Manchester United in 2004, substituting for skipper Dennis Wise.

— OUT FOR THE COUNT —

'And I suppose they [Spurs] are nearer to being out of the FA Cup now than at any other time since the first half of this season – when they weren't ever in it anyway.'
– John Motson!

— WEMBLEY SEMI —

The first time a semi-final was played at Wembley was in 1991, when Arsenal and Spurs were drawn together and 78,000 North Londoners travelled the short distance to watch Spurs beat their old rivals from Highbury.

— TOP GIANT-KILLERS —

Yeovil Town are the team that no opponent should want to meet in the Cup draw. Although they were promoted to Football League One in 2005, the Glovers beat 20 Football League teams when they were not members themselves.

— SHOOT-OUT —

Penalty shoot-outs were introduced to settle Cup ties after a second drawn match from the 1991–92 season. Before that, Birmingham City had beaten Stoke City on penalties in the third-place play-off in 1972.

— BROTHERS UNITED —

Gary and Philip Neville were in Manchester United's victorious squads of 1996, 1999 and 2004 – the first brothers to win the FA Cup together since Brian and Jimmy Greenhoff, also for United, in 1977.

— WELCOME BACK TO WEMBLEY —

After an absence of four years, the FA Cup final returns to its spiritual home, Wembley Stadium, in 2006.

Much has changed since the days of the legendary Twin Towers. Indeed, many believe the new stadium will be the finest footballing arena on the planet.

The statistics are certainly impressive:

- With 90,000 seats the new Wembley will be the largest all-covered football stadium in the world. There will be no obstructed views.

- The arch is 133 metres above the level of the external concourse.

- The roof rises to 52 metres above the pitch. This compares to the Twin Towers of the old stadium reaching 35 metres.

- The new Wembley has a circumference of 1 kilometre.

- The London Eye could fit between the top of the arch and the pitch.

- The new roof is more than 11 acres in expanse, of which four acres are moveable.

- The rows of seating, if placed end to end, would stretch 54 kilometres.

- 4,000 separate piles form the foundations. The deepest of these, at 35 metres, is as deep as the Twin Towers were tall.

- There are 35 miles of heavy-duty power cables.

- With a span of 315 metres, the arch is the longest single-span roof structure in the world.

- With a diameter of 7.4 metres, the arch is wide enough for a Channel Tunnel train to run through.

- 90,000 cubic metres of concrete and 23,000 tonnes of steel have been used in the construction of the new stadium.

- The roof weighs almost 7,000 tonnes.

- At peak construction there were more than 2,000 people working on site.

- The new pitch is four metres lower than the previous pitch.

- Each of the two giant screens is the size of 600 domestic television sets.

- The new Wembley encloses 4,000,000 cubic metres inside its walls and under its roof. This is the equivalent of 25,000 double-decker buses or 7 billion pints of milk.

- The total length of the escalators is the same as a 400-metre running track.

- There are 2,618 toilets.

- There is more leg room for every seat in the new Wembley than there was in the royal box of the old stadium.

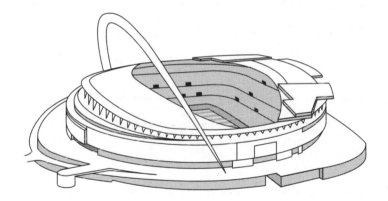

— WALLY DEFIES THE YEARS —

Newcastle United right-back Wally Hampson was an old head on old shoulders as his side beat Aston Villa 2–0 in the FA Cup final of 1924. At 41 years and eight months, he was, and remains, the oldest player to appear in a final.

— FA CUP WINS —

11	Manchester United	2004, 1999, 1996, 1994, 1990, 1985, 1983, 1977, 1963, 1948, 1909
10	Arsenal	2005, 2003, 2002, 1998, 1993, 1979, 1971, 1950, 1936, 1930
8	Tottenham Hotspur	1991, 1982, 1981, 1967, 1962, 1961, 1921, 1901
7	Aston Villa	1957, 1920, 1913, 1905, 1897, 1895, 1887
6	Liverpool	2001, 1992, 1989, 1986, 1974, 1965
	Newcastle United	1955, 1952, 1951, 1932, 1924, 1910
	Blackburn Rovers	1928, 1891, 1890, 1886, 1885, 1884
5	Everton	1995, 1984, 1966, 1933, 1906
	West Bromwich Albion	1968, 1954, 1931, 1892, 1888
	The Wanderers	1878, 1877, 1876, 1873, 1872
4	Manchester City	1969, 1956, 1934, 1904
	Wolverhampton Wanderers	1960, 1949, 1908, 1893
	Bolton Wanderers	1958, 1929, 1926, 1923
	Sheffield United	1925, 1915, 1902, 1899
3	Chelsea	2000, 1997, 1970
	West Ham United	1980, 1975, 1964
	Sheffield Wednesday	1935, 1907, 1896
2	Sunderland	1973, 1937
	Nottingham Forest	1959, 1898
	Preston North End	1938, 1889
	Bury	1903, 1900
	Old Etonians	1882, 1879
1	Wimbledon	1988
	Coventry City	1987
	Ipswich Town	1978
	Southampton	1976
	Leeds United	1972
	Blackpool	1953
	Charlton Athletic	1947
	Derby County	1946
	Portsmouth	1939

Cardiff City	1927
Huddersfield Town	1922
Burnley	1914
Barnsley	1912
Bradford City	1911
Notts County	1894
Blackburn Olympic	1883
Old Carthusians	1881
Clapham Rovers	1880
Royal Engineers	1875
Oxford University	1874

— GOING, GOING, GONE —

The first noteworthy auction of football memorabilia was held by Christie's in Glasgow in 1989 when a Cup final medal belonging to Arsenal's Alex James went under the hammer. Valued at £1,000, it was sold for £5,000 – and today would probably be worth as much as £50,000.

— RADIO ON —

The first FA Cup final to be broadcast live on the radio was the 1927 game between Arsenal and Cardiff City. The commentator was George Allison, who later became Arsenal's manager. His co-commentator was Derek McCulloch, who would find his own fame and fortune subsequently, as Uncle Mac on BBC Radio's *Children's Hour*.

— HOW THE OTHER HALF LIVE —

'He showed us around the ground, let us into both changing rooms, told us to talk to any players we wanted, get their autographs and their shirts.'
– Scunthorpe's Paul Hayes meets Chelsea boss Jose Mourinho prior to their 2005 third-round tie.

— BROTHERS IN GLOVES —

Goalkeeping brothers John and Charles Sutcliffe hold the record for the longest period between two brothers appearing in FA Cup finals. John kept goal for Bolton Wanderers when they lost to Notts County in 1894, then Charles turned out for Sheffield United 31 years later when they beat Cardiff City in 1925.

— IN THE BEGINNING —

The first Football Association Challenge Cup final took place on Saturday, 16 March 1872 – but if you'd been among the crowd of 2,000 who had paid the extortionate entrance fee of a shilling (5p) to attend the match at London's Kennington Oval you would have struggled to recognise anything that was going on.

For a start, the match was played without crossbars or goal-nets. There were no such things as free-kicks or penalties, and the pitch markings did not include a centre-circle or a halfway line.

There were, at least, two teams.

Wanderers boasted the pick of all the best players to attend public school and university. Captained by FA secretary Charles Alcock – who a year earlier had proposed that a Challenge Cup should be competed for – the team had no fewer than six future internationals in their ranks. These included the famous R W S Vidal from Westminster School, known as 'The Prince of Dribblers'.

Despite this array of talent, they had scraped through to the final, only getting past Queen's Park in the semi because the Scottish side had insufficient funds to stay in London for a replay.

Perhaps because of this it was the Royal Engineers, a team of rock-hard squaddies from Chatham barracks in Kent, who were favourites to win.

The Engineers were dealt a grievous blow after ten minutes, however, when their centre-half Lieutenant Cresswell suffered a broken collarbone. Although he manfully stayed on the pitch (there were, of course, no substitutes – nor would there be until 1968), a few minutes later 'The Prince of Dribblers' lived up to his soubriquet with a mazy 40-yard run which unstitched the Engineers' defence and allowed Morton Peto Betts – curiously playing under the pseudonym A H Chequer – to fire home from an acute angle.

From then on it was one-way traffic, and observers were generally in agreement that the Engineers were lucky to escape a hiding.

It was perhaps fitting that this inaugural final should feature an act of giant-killing. The Wanderers, however, would go on to win another four finals and become not only the first winners of the Cup, but the first side to dominate the competition.

— TO LOVE, HONOUR, AND WATCH THE SPURS —

In 1997 avid Spurs fans Neil Campbell and Joan Dowey were married at St Margaret's Church, Wellington. Immediately afterwards, and still wearing their wedding finery, they were chauffeured to Edgar Street, where their beloved team were in FA Cup third-round action against Hereford United. The game finished 1–1, but Neil and Joan were able to see Spurs win the replay 5–1 at White Hart Lane before going on honeymoon.

— CUP OF PLENTY —

The FA Cup has always been popular with fans and players alike – but, as this diagram shows, such is the financial benefit of progressing through the rounds that the competition is also much loved by impoverished chairmen.

— CUP BOMBSHELL —

In 1915 Britain was at war, but the FA Cup continued. A Parliamentary debate about dud shells failing to explode on the battlefield concluded that one of the reasons for the malfunction was that too many munitions workers were more interested in the fate of their local teams than in fitting detonators correctly. As a result the FA decreed that no games were to be played near munitions factories during working hours.

— MAGIC PREPARATIONS —

Many teams claim to have their own pre-match rituals and in the FA Cup some are more successful than others. In 1939 Scarborough reached the third round, claiming the secret to their success was regular seaweed baths for the players. By contrast, King's Lynn reckoned that a pre-match meal of steak washed down with egg-nog would help them over-come Southend United in 1968. It didn't, and they lost 9–0.

— WOKING HIT THE BIG TIME —

'We had 10,000 fans here, young lads were asking for an autograph and old men wanted to shake me by the hand. I mean, who the hell am I?'
– Woking skipper Adie Cowler after the non-League part-timers from Surrey had been beaten 1–0 by Everton at Goodison Park in the fourth round in 1991. In the previous round, they had caused a sensation by trouncing West Bromwich Albion 4–2 at the Hawthorns.

— THE END OF THE AMATEUR —

The 1881 final between Old Carthusians and Old Etonians was the last between amateur sides. Wanderers had scratched from that year's competition and neither Oxford nor Cambridge Universities were among the 63 entrants.

— YOU NEED HANDS . . . —

Prior to the 1979 FA Cup final against Arsenal, Manchester United boss Dave Sexton came up with a novel way of encouraging his team to win the match. On the way to Wembley Stadium on the afternoon of the big game, Sexton put a Max Bygraves album on the bus cassette player. 'We play Max on the way to matches as an incentive to the players,' Sexton told bemused reporters. 'If we lose, we have to listen to it on the way back.'

It must have been a very long journey back indeed as United were beaten 3–2 in a dramatic showpiece won by Alan Sunderland's last-gasp strike.

— SIX-GOAL BORE —

Bury's six-goal thrashing of Derby County in 1903 continues to excite statisticians as it remains the record margin of victory in FA Cup finals. But at the time, the match was regarded as being one of the most boring and one-sided finals in the short history of the competition.

Derby were dire that day, but it still took Bury 20 minutes before skipper George Ross opened the scoring. After that, it was carnage with four goals being scored inside just 11 minutes at the start of the second half.

To celebrate their win – and the fact that they had now scored 10 unanswered goals in two final appearances – the Lancastrians treated themselves to a slap-up meal at the Trocadero in London's Piccadilly Circus.

— A GOOD DECISION —

Manchester United's first Cup final win in 1909 hung on a contentious but ultimately match-turning decision by skipper Charlie Roberts. United's influential inside-left Sandy Turnbull was struggling with a knee injury but Roberts opted for a gamble. 'Let him play,' he said. 'He might get a goal, and if he does we can carry him.' Sure enough, Turnbull scored the only goal of the game after 22 minutes, securing victory against Bristol City at Crystal Palace. Tragically, he was killed in action five years later on the battlefields of northern France.

— A TIMELY BOOT —

The 1912 final between Barnsley and West Bromwich Albion was a dour affair, eventually settled by a single extra-time goal by the Yorkshiremen in the replay. They owed their win in no small part to the quick thinking of defender Jack Glendinning. Off the pitch, receiving treatment to an injured toe, Glendinning watched in horror as West Brom's Ben Shearman broke clear, rounded the 'keeper and struck the ball goalwards. Scrambling to his feet, and wearing just one boot, Glendinning raced back on to the pitch to hoof the ball clear in the nick of time. This incident led to the rule that a player who leaves the field must receive the referee's permission before returning to the fray.

The winning goal was equally bizarre. With just two minutes remaining in extra time, the ball fell to Barnsley's Harry Tufnell who found himself through on goal with only Albion defender Jesse Pennington to beat. A professional foul was required to stop Tufnell, but the gentlemanly Pennington refused to commit such an act and the goal was duly scored.

— WHAT A NERVE! —

Prior to the 1926 final between Bolton and Manchester City, fans were somewhat surprised to see Bolton players including David Jack and Ted Vizard tipping packets of a suspicious-looking white powder down their throats. This was the Lancashire club's renowned 'nerve' powder – in reality nothing more than a glucose-based mixture designed to settle the stomach and provide energy. And it worked! Jack and Vizard combined to score the only goal of the game, with Jack putting the ball in the net for Bolton's second Cup final win in three years.

— PRE-MATCH WORD OF WARNING —

'Sunderland!'
– Manchester United boss Tommy Docherty's pre-match pep talk to his side prior to their 1976 Cup final against Second Division Southampton. But, like Leeds three years earlier, the First Division giants were beaten 1–0 by the minnows from the south coast.

— CLEVER DICK —

Goalkeeper Dick Pym had the remarkable distinction of not conceding a goal in each of his three Cup finals for Bolton Wanderers. Pym was no stranger to nets, however, having turned his back on the family fishing business for a career at Burnden Park.

— THE VOICE OF REASON —

'Take no notice of the milk-and-water boys who want us to play our soccer in blue bows and ballet shoes. All over the country you can hear them whining their annual Cup final anthem: "We want substitutes!"

'They are soccer's fifth column and they are doing the rounds trying to kid you that you don't get your money's worth at Wembley, that it isn't right for a team like Nottingham Forest to play a man short for an hour. And in doing so they will rob Nottingham Forest of their finest hour!

'If ever there was a soccer Dunkirk we saw it on Saturday, with ten men running themselves into treacherous turf while covering up for one of their star players, who was sweating it out in hospital.'
– Laurie Pignon of the *Daily Sketch* in 1959 after Forest's Roy Dwight (suffering a broken leg) had become the sixth man in seven years to be badly injured during an FA Cup final.

— REFFING CHEEK! —

At the end of their epic 1978 Cup triumph over mighty Arsenal, the elated Ipswich Town side were beaten to the lap of honour by referee Derek Nippard and his linesmen. Nippard, 47, took the opportunity to celebrate his own landmark – it was the end of his last season as a League referee.

— RECORD CROWD —

The 95,000 people who crammed into Wembley Stadium to watch Cardiff City play Sheffield United in the 1925 final were the largest crowd ever to watch a Welsh team in action either in football or rugby union.

— BOOTS 'N' ALL —

Fulham's one and only FA Cup final appearance against West Ham in 1975 was very nearly kicked into touch before it started. On the day before the match, boot manufacturer Stylo decided to issue an injunction preventing Alan Mullery's side from wearing any other brand of footwear at Wembley.

The firm claimed Fulham were in breach of an agreement in which they had agreed to wear Stylo boots for the entire 1974–75 season. This was after several of the team were spotted wearing different brands in a League match at Bristol City the week before.

As a result, the night before the final a solicitor representing Stylo was instructed to go to the team hotel in Hertfordshire and serve writs to all 14 members of the first-team squad. 'We've just changed the formation,' Fulham centre-half Bobby Moore noted dryly. 'We've got an outside-writ, an inside-writ and a writ-half.'

The matter was eventually resolved when Mullery, Moore et al walked on to the Wembley turf wearing Stylo boots. Their opponents, West Ham, were wearing Adidas boots after clinching a lucrative contract worth £3,500.